1,001+ Housewife How-To's®:

Household Hints to Help Homebodies Clean, Cook,
Organize, Save Money and More!

by

Katie Berry

Table of Contents

INTRODUCTION

This book is not just for housewives! It's not just for homeowners, either. The 1,001+ tips in this book are for anyone who finds cooking, cleaning, doing laundry, organizing and removing clutter, or tending the lawn and garden to be a chore.

So why the "housewife" part in the title? Because I'm a housewife and these are my how-to's! It's also the name of my blog, *Housewife How-To's®*, where I teach people to cook, clean, get organized, do laundry and save money... without losing their minds.

Whether you are a man or a woman, married or single, a homeowner or a renter, these tips can help you spend less time and money maintaining your *stuff* so you can spend your time doing the things you love.

A WORD ABOUT COMMON SENSE

"Common sense is not so common." - Voltaire

Common sense means using good judgment. Sadly, as Voltaire noted, not many people have it or use it. Don't be one of those people! When following the hints in this book, please exercise common sense:

- Spot test stain removal techniques to make sure an item is colorfast.

- Don't use rubbing alcohol, ammonia or other flammable substances near open flames, including cigarettes, candles and pilot lights.

- Don't mix water and electricity. That also means: don't touch things that use electricity if you're wet.

- Be careful with sharp stuff.

- Get help if something is heavy.

- Don't stand on the top of a ladder. In fact, stay a couple of steps down... and have someone nearby if you can.

- Don't combine bleach or ammonia with each other OR with other cleaners.

Yes, these things seem kind of obvious when you're reading them. Unfortunately, they still need to be said.

COOKING

Baking

Don't pay high grocery store prices for colored sugar. Make your own by placing sugar in a plastic bag, adding a few drops of your favorite food coloring, and shaking it until evenly colored.

Want a really flaky pie crust? Keep everything cold: cut butter into cubes then chill it; use ice water; chill the pie tin ahead of time and again after lining it with crust.

Wipe beaters and mixing bowl with a little white vinegar before you whip egg whites. This will remove any lingering oils that keep those stiff peaks from forming.

If your recipe calls for room temperature eggs but you're in a hurry, get them warmed up quickly by putting them in a bowl of lukewarm water for 10 minutes.

Not great at decorating cakes or cookies with piped icing? Draw the design on with a toothpick first then follow with the icing to get professional-looking results.

Make sure you have two sets of measuring spoons and, ideally, measuring cups. Having one available for wet ingredients and another for dry can save time when you're cooking.

Get a lighter, homemade look from store-bought frosting by whipping it with a mixer. It will double in volume and spread easier, too.

Need to measure something sticky like honey or peanut butter? Soak the measuring cup in very hot water first and the measured ingredient will slip right out.

Use unsalted butter to grease baking pans. Butter containing salt can actually make foods stick.

Coat your stand mixer's dough hook with a very light layer of neutral-tasting oil to keep dough from climbing out of the bowl as you mix.

Keep cookies from spreading too thin as they bake by chilling the dough for 20 minutes first.

Those slits in the top crust of fruit pies aren't just for decoration: they allow steam to escape as the pie bakes so the top crust doesn't puff up and then collapse.

Rolling pie crust between two sheets of wax or parchment paper makes it easy to turn the crust into the pan: just lift off the top sheet, invert the dough onto the pie tin, and peel the paper away.

Crack eggs into a small bowl one at a time and add them individually to whatever you're cooking. This way you won't ruin the whole recipe if an egg is rotten and it will be easier to fish out any fragments of shell, too.

Unless your recipe directs otherwise, all of your ingredients (including eggs and milk) should be at room temperature when baking.

To keep layer cakes from bulging as they bake, lower the oven temperature from 350° to 325°. You'll need to bake it 10 or so minutes longer but the layers will be flat and the texture will be just as fine.

Take your time when creaming sugar and butter together for baked goods. You want to beat them for 3 to 5 minutes until they're fluffy so your baked goods will be, too.

Use the rack on the lowest position in your oven when baking pies to form a good, golden brown bottom crust.

Old baking soda can keep baked goods from rising properly. Replace yours every six months.

Make your own dark brown sugar by mixing 1/2 cup molasses with 1 cup of white sugar. For golden brown sugar, reduce the molasses to 1/4 cup.

Before you fill a pie crust with a cream or pudding filling, spread a layer of powdered sugar on the bottom of the crust first. The sugar will form a barrier that keeps your crust from getting soggy without changing the taste of your dessert.

Drape a towel over the top of your stand mixer's bowl when combining powdery things like flour and your counters will stay clean.

If there's not enough batter to fill all the holes in your cupcake or muffin tin be sure to fill empty ones with hot water so your pans don't scorch.

Get a straight, clean cut on cakes and soft cheeses with unflavored dental floss. Hold it tautly between your hands and saw while gently pressing down. Wipe the floss as needed so it stays clean.

Reduce the fat in your baked goods without affecting flavor or texture by replacing up to half of the oil in a recipe with unsweetened applesauce.

Minimize mess and waste when baking by keeping a brand new powder puff in your flour container. Use it to dust a light coating over cutting boards, counters and rolling pins.

Get a glossy finish to frosted cakes by blasting them with a blow-dryer for 10 seconds.

Never twist the cutter when you're making biscuits: that pinches the dough together so you won't get flaky, light layers.

Loosen a cake that's stuck to the bottom of the pan by dipping just the lowest inch of the pan in a sink of hot water for 30 seconds. The cake will come out easily when you invert it on a baking rack.

If homemade dough keeps shrinking when you're trying to pat or roll it into place, give it a rest for 10 minutes to weaken the gluten strands so it stretches easier.

Use your hands, not a rolling pin, when shaping pizza dough. Rolling bursts the air bubbles that give a lighter texture.

You can get a crispy bottom to your homemade pizza crust by oiling the baking sheet. This helps fry the crust bottom as the pie bakes.

Beverages

Keep your lemonade frosty without watering it down by freezing some as ice cubes. You can use the same trick with iced tea, juices, even coffee.

Plop some frozen grapes into your wine glass to keep it cold without diluting the taste. Or try frozen citrus slices in red wine for a neat twist! (No pun intended.)

You don't have to wait for a sunny day to make "sun tea": add the tea bags to cool water and leave the container on a windowsill or even your counter for the day.

If the cork crumbles when you're opening a bottle of wine, strain the bits by pouring the wine through a coffee filter.

Can't wait for that bottle of wine or pop to chill in the refrigerator? Try this: fill the bottom third of a deep bowl with ice then sprinkle on some salt. Add the bottle then more layers of ice and salt. Now add some water. The salt lowers the freezing point of water so the combination speedily chills your beverage.

Add clean crushed eggshells with your ground coffee when you brew your next pot. The eggshells counteract the coffee's acid and give it a sweeter, milder taste.

If you can't get the cork back into the wine bottle, try soaking it in hot water for a few minutes and it will squeeze into place.

Like sugar and cream in your coffee? Freeze spoonfuls of whipped cream on a baking sheet. Drop one or two in your java to sweeten and cool it while adding cream, too.

Condiments, Sauces and Gravies

Hate waiting for the ketchup to pour? Insert a knife or drinking straw into the bottle and pull it out to make your condiment flow faster.

If you don't like the taste of capers, try substituting minced green olives in recipes instead.

Keep your homemade pesto bright green by adding basil as the final ingredient and then only blending it in the food processor until it is just mixed.

There are many things besides basil you can make pesto from. Try using parsley, cilantro, even arugula or Swiss chard.

Give your beef gravy a bold flavor by substituting leftover coffee for half the broth.

Since pine nuts are so expensive, try substituting walnuts or sunflower seeds when making pesto. Almonds work, too!

When making homemade mayonnaise, don't use expensive extra-virgin olive oil; the taste is too bold. Go for the oil described as "extra-light *tasting*" and you'll get a smooth, delicious mayonnaise.

Don't season gravy until it's simmered and reduced. Too early and you'll wind up with an over-seasoned mess.

Don't toss scorched gravy. Transfer it to a different pan, add a pinch of sugar, and stir well. No more burned taste!

Cooking Tools and Gadgets

Egg slicers aren't just for eggs! Use them to evenly slice mushrooms, strawberries, pickles and olives.

Fill reusable bottles with water, leaving 1 inch of headspace, and freeze them. Add to lunch boxes and they'll keep food cool until lunch time.

Opening the oven door drops the temperature by up to 50°F every time, which means your food won't cook evenly and will take longer to be ready. Use a timer, remote thermometer or oven light instead.

Pastry scrapers can do double-duty in the kitchen carrying minced herbs or chopped vegetables between the cutting board and pan.

Short on counter space in the kitchen? Pull open a drawer and rest a cutting board on top of it for more surface area while you're working.

Sliding knives in and out of a knife block can dull the blades. Keep yours sharp by storing them with the non-cutting side down.

Slip your kitchen's TV remote into a plastic bag when you're cooking so you can adjust volume and change channels without getting food on the buttons.

Want to heat two bowls at the same time in the microwave? Turn a coffee mug upside down and put one bowl on top of it, the other on the microwave turntable. This works with plates, too.

Resist the urge to dump all of your all ingredients in the slow cooker at once. Dairy will just curdle and look unappetizing, so wait to stir it in during the last 15-20 minutes of cooking.

Don't touch that slow cooker lid! Every time you open the lid you let heat escape and your food will need at least 20 more minutes to finish.

Keep cutting boards from sliding around on slick kitchen counters as you're chopping by placing them on a damp kitchen towel.

Pastry tips make it easy to remove pits from cherries and olives: just poke the tip through from the bottom of the fruit and push the pit right out.

Potato ricers aren't just for making the best mashed potatoes ever: use them to squeeze sliced citrus fruit and you'll get every drop with none of the pulp.

There's no need to buy a gadget to hull strawberries. Just poke a drinking straw through them from the tip to the stem to remove the hull.

Cooking with Kids

Help kids develop safe knife skills by letting them chop lettuce with a plastic knife. Unlike their metal counterparts, plastic knives won't cause lettuce to turn brown.

Keep a bowl of soapy water handy and teach kids to clean as they go while cooking. It's a great life skill that reduces kitchen messes.

Try to schedule early cooking experiences on the weekends, rather than a weeknight when you're busy and on a schedule. Kids learn best without pressure and you'll stress less about the messes when you can take your time.

Have kids snip herbs: show them how to strip the leaves from the stems and drop them into a coffee mug. Give your little one a pair of scissors and the mug then let them snip the herbs with the scissor tips.

Let kids peel potatoes. Stick a corkscrew in the end of the potato to make it easier for their little hands to hold.

When you're first teaching your kids to cook, set them up a cooking station of their own at the table or on an end of the counter, somewhere away from heat. Not only is it safer but you'll be able to work without tripping over them.

If you're going to have your kid stir ingredients together, be sure the bowl is DEEP. Kids love to stir vigorously like they see on cartoons but with a shallow bowl the ingredients will go flying all over your kitchen.

Cooking is a great way to teach kids a variety of things. Pick a country and research its cuisine at the library or online. What's life like for kids there? Where is it on the map? Learn how to say your names in that country's language. Listen to the country's folk music while you cook.

When cooking on the stove top, make sure handles are turned to the side and not sticking out over the edge of the stove. This keeps little hands from being able to grab them and bigger hips from knocking them off.

Dairy Foods

Cottage cheese, sour cream and yogurt all stay fresh longer when stored upside down. Make sure the lid is on properly first!

If you can't finish that gallon of milk before the expiration date, try freezing what's left in ice cube trays. Use the defrosted cubes when you're baking or cooking.

Grating cheese yourself saves quite a bit of money: an 8-ounce block is usually half the cost of 8-ounces preshredded. It melts better, too, because the additives used to keep commercially grated cheese from clumping also make it tougher.

Keep butter from sliding all over the dish by running the butter dish under hot water then putting the stick of butter on it and popping it into the fridge. The residual heat will melt the butter onto the dish just a little, but once cooled the butter will stay put.

Make clarified butter (or ghee) in large batches using your slow cooker: add 2 pounds and set it on low. Scoop away the milk solids that rise to the top and strain the melted butter through cheesecloth to remove the rest. Store in jars in the refrigerator for two months, or freeze it for up to a year.

Freshly grated Parmesan cheese from a wedge tastes and melts so much better than the pre-grated stuff (which is coated in additives to prevent clumping). Grate yours all at once and store in airtight containers, or grate it just as needed. When you get to the rind, toss it in soup to add another layer of flavor.

Make grating cheese faster by freezing it for 15 minutes first.

Rub a little oil or butter on your cheese grater before grating. It speeds things up, and also makes the grater easier to clean.

Prolong the life of expensive cheeses by rubbing a thin layer of butter on the cut end then wrapping the whole thing in parchment paper followed by aluminum foil. Store it with your vegetables in the crisper drawer if you can.

Stock up when blocks of cheese go on sale, grate them, and stash the grated cheese in the freezer. Pre-frozen cheese doesn't taste good on crackers but it tastes just as good in casseroles or on nachos.

Trying to spread cold butter on warm toast just makes a mess. Use a vegetable peeler to shave thin slices off the butter and they'll spread easily.

Eggs

Cook ingredients before adding them to omelets or scrambled eggs. Using raw ingredients means they'll release their moisture while they cook, turning your omelet or scrambled eggs soggy.

Egg whites are easiest to separate when they're cold, but once separated be sure to let them reach room temperature so they whip up higher and faster.

Get the fluffiest scrambled eggs by whisking in a small pinch of baking soda.

Don't add liquid to eggs when making an omelet. The only reason to do so is to slow the cooking process down, but you'll get a better omelet by simply turning down the heat.

Peeling hard boiled eggs can be a nuisance. Try adding 1 tablespoon of vinegar and a large pinch of salt to the water as they boil and those shells will slip right off.

Remember the opposites rule to peel hardboiled eggs easily: crack the shells then run warm eggs under cold water, and cold eggs under warm water. The shells will slip away.

Stir eggs as you boil them to keep the yolks centered.

Stock up on eggs when they're on sale, then crack them individually into ice cube trays. Stir gently with a toothpick, freeze, and stash the cubes in a resealable freezer bag. Use the egg cubes for baking or in casseroles.

To reheat hard boiled eggs, peel them and poke through with a toothpick then microwave for 20 seconds. Or put the peeled eggs in a bowl of hot water for 2 minutes.

Food Storage

Add a stalk of celery to the bread bag if it's starting to get stale and the celery's moisture will make your bread soft again.

Toss bread at the first sign of mold. Even if you only see it on one end, mold spores can work their way through the bread and ruin the whole thing.

A food vacuum sealer is worth every penny, especially if you buy the attachment that also seals jars. Frozen foods last almost indefinitely once vacuum sealed, and leftovers stay good in the fridge three times as long.

Don't need the whole can of tomato paste? Cut the bottom off and stick what's left in the freezer for an hour. Once it is firm, run a table knife or small spatula around the can and pop the frozen paste into a bag to use later.

Mince excess fresh herbs and stir them into softened butter, then shape into a log and wrap tightly with plastic wrap. Store this compound butter in the freezer and grate shavings onto grilled meats, vegetables and fish. It's delicious on toast and bagels, too!

Keep raw meats in the lowest drawer of your refrigerator, ideally in plastic bags to catch drips. Higher up in the fridge compromises the safety of all of your food if their packages leak.

Never store milk or eggs in the refrigerator door *even if* there's a space for it. For food safety, it's important these items remain at proper temperatures, but that doesn't happen if they're exposed to warm air every time someone opens the fridge. The best spot is at the back of the lowest shelf.

Leftover chocolate pudding can make a delicious frozen treat. Put it into an ice cube tray, cover tightly with plastic wrap, and poke a toothpick into each cube before freezing. Remove the plastic carefully and you've got mini-pudding pops.

Refrigerating tossed salads in your salad spinner can help them last longer. Each day, pull the basket out and wipe the bowl dry to keep your greens crisped for up to a week.

Preserve fresh herbs from your garden by mincing them and then putting them in an ice cube tray. Top with water or olive oil and freeze. Now you can drop herb-flavored cubes into soups and stews to enjoy that fresh taste all year long.

Store heads of lettuce in brown paper bags in the crisper drawer. The paper will absorb excess moisture so your lettuce stays crisp longer.

Use dry erase markers to write the dates on containers of leftovers so you know how long they've been in your fridge.

Tomato sauce, pickled foods, and citrus are all highly acidic. Don't wrap foods containing these ingredients in aluminum foil, or the acid will react with the wrap and change your leftovers' taste.

Tuck an apple slice under the dome with your cake to keep your dessert moist for days.

Why buy frozen waffles or pancakes when it's so easy to freeze your own? Make extras using your favorite recipe and place them on baking sheets so they're not touching. Freeze until solid, and then pop them into freezer bags. You can warm them in the microwave or toaster oven for wholesome hot breakfasts on school days.

Frozen Foods

No one likes finding their favorite ice cream covered in frozen crystals. Cover it with a piece of wax paper before putting the lid on to keep crystals from forming.

Pop a mini-marshmallow into the bottom of ice cream cones to stop drips.

Use real cream and whole milk when making frozen desserts at home. The chemical stabilizers used to keep half-and-half from separating can destroy your homemade ice cream.

Make your own "TV Dinners" for healthy, convenient frozen meals. Just put leftovers on a sturdy paper plate with dividers, then wrap tightly in plastic wrap followed by foil. To serve, remove the foil and reheat the whole plate in the microwave straight from the freezer.

Artificial sweeteners can keep frozen treats from freezing properly. Use honey or stevia instead.

Some things, like frozen pizzas, are best baked directly on the oven racks. Keep them from leaving burned food on the bottom of your oven by placing a sheet of aluminum foil on another rack positioned below your food.

Frying

Always run your range hood fan when frying foods. Even fans built into microwaves over the stove still filter the grease and some cooking odors out of the air, along with particles created by the cooking process which can irritate lungs.

Breading meats and vegetables right after they come out of the fridge can lead to a soggy crust because the food will develop a layer of moisture as it comes to room temperature. To avoid this, remove food from the fridge and then wait for 30 minutes before breading. If you're concerned about food safety, check the internal temperature of your food while frying and you'll be fine.

Find out if oil is ready for frying by sticking the handle of a wooden spoon into it. When the oil is hot enough you'll see bubbles form and start rolling up the spoon handle.

For crispy "oven-fried" fare, place food on a baking rack set atop a cookie sheet to let the heat circulate and crisp all sides of your food as it cooks.

Heating oil to the proper temperature is important when frying food. If it's not hot enough your food will soak up too much oil, and if it's too hot outside will burn before the inside is fully cooked.

Instead of putting fried foods directly on paper towels after cooking, place the towel beneath a baking rack. The rack will keep food a bit higher so air can circulate, which means the fried coating will stay nice and crisp.

Keep grease from splattering all over your kitchen by covering the pan with a metal colander as you cook.

Let breading rest on food at least 15 minutes before frying for the crispiest crust.

Grains and Legumes

Add a squirt of lemon juice to the water when you're cooking rice. Not only will it brighten the grains, it will keep them from sticking together.

Always rinse quinoa well with cold water before cooking to remove the bitter coating on the seeds.

If you scorch the rice, you can get rid of the burned taste out by removing it from heat then placing a slice of bread on top of it and closing the lid for 5 minutes. Toss the bread, fluff the grains and serve.

Meat isn't the only thing that needs to rest after cooking for best flavor. Let grains finish steaming without opening the lid for a few minutes after removing from heat. Fluff with a fork before serving.

Change the water a few times when you're soaking beans. This removes some of the raffinose that causes gas.

Never stir rice while it's cooking, or you'll just make it gummy.

Don't use instant rice in meals you plan to freeze since it will turn into a tasteless mush as it defrosts. Use regular rice instead, and opt for brown rice for the best nutrition.

Rinse dried beans well in cool water before cooking to remove dust. As a bonus, this helps reduce the gas you'll have after eating them.

Take the time to pick over dried beans before cooking. Farmers use massive machines to harvest them in bulk, which often means small rocks and twigs get caught in the mix. You don't want to break a tooth just because you were in a hurry!

To make gluten-free "bread crumbs" run brown rice cereal or GF pretzels in your food processor, then follow the rest of your recipe.

Herbs, Spices, Extracts and Seasonings

Add a few grains of rice to your salt shaker to prevent clumping.

If your honey has formed crystals, you don't have to pour it out. Put the container in a bowl of hot water for a few minutes then stir, changing water repeatedly until the honey is liquid again.

Four things primarily affect the flavor of foods: fat, acid, sweetness and salt. If you're not happy with the flavor of a soup, try adjusting the flavor profile. To add fat, use butter, cream or even coconut milk. For acid, use a splash of white or red wine vinegar, or a squeeze of citrus. Sweet can be found in agave nectar, honey, and coconut or brown sugar. And, of course, there's always salt.

Make your own vanilla extract by steeping 4 scraped vanilla beans in 3 ounces of vodka. Store this in a dark bottle and shake regularly. Four weeks later, strain it and it's ready to use.

An easy way to reduce your salt intake is by plugging one of the holes on your salt shaker with a piece of rice.

Always use cold water to rinse lettuces, greens and herbs. Warm water not only wilts them but, in the case of herbs, washes away some of the plant oils that give them flavor.

Don't throw away empty peppercorn grinders. Refill them with coriander or celery seeds, dried citrus peel, or dried hot peppers. A few twists can add amazing flavor to your food.

Garlic's pungency can vary over the year and between varieties, so a recipe that calls for three cloves might only need one. Rather than risk overpowering your meal, add garlic a little at a time. You can always add more if needed.

If you can't use all of the lemongrass you bought at the store for that one recipe, chop the rest then steep it in hot water for 15 minutes. This makes a delicious lemony-flavored tea to drink or to use in place of water in baked goods.

Make fresh herbs last longer by snipping the stems and putting them in a glass with an inch or two of water. Cover them loosely with a plastic produce bag to form a mini-greenhouse environment and store this in the refrigerator. Be sure to change the water every few days and you can keep them good for well over a week.

To mince garlic quickly with a fork, turn the utensil over and "grate" garlic cloves against the tines.

Swap fresh herbs for dried in your recipes (and vice versa) by using 3 times as many fresh herbs as you would dry.

Most recipes call for just a little bit of fresh ginger. Rather than letting the rest of the root spoil in the fridge, freeze it. Next time you need ginger, just break off a piece to defrost. The rest will stay good for up to a year.

Peel several cloves of garlic quickly by shaking them between two bowls or in a large tightly-closed jar for 30 seconds.

Use a garlic press to "mince" ginger and you'll get the entire flavor with half of the work.

Shaking spices from the jar over a simmering pot can spoil them; measure with a spoon away from the cooking food.

Help kids learn proper portion sizes by leaving a serving-sized measuring cup in the cereal box. Over time, they'll learn how to eyeball the right portion and you'll save a small fortune on cereal.

Kitchen Scraps and Leftovers

Save the green tops of beets, turnips, radishes and carrots. Cook them in a little olive oil with garlic, or mince and add them to soups, stews or tossed salads.

Add a mug filled with water to the microwave when you reheat pizza to keep the crust soft.

Did someone forget to close the bag of tortilla chips? Don't throw them out! Add crushed tortilla chips, salsa and grated cheese to scrambled eggs and you've got a quick version of a beloved Mexican breakfast called "Migas". Yum!

Save bread heels in the freezer to make homemade croutons and breadcrumbs.

Save vegetable scraps, even the ones left on your kid's plate at dinner, in a large container in the freezer. When it's full, tip the vegetables into a stock pot and cover with water. Let simmer 2 to 4 hours then strain for homemade vegetable stock.

Cooking Meats and Fish

Bone-in meat cooks slower so it stays moister. The bone enhances the meaty flavor, too.

Baking bacon ensures every piece is fully cooked, and you can cook more at the same time. Use a broiling pan or a baking rack placed over a rimmed baking sheet and cook it at 375° for 10-15 minutes, rotating the sheet halfway through.

Browning meat doesn't just keep it from turning an unappetizing gray. Browning develops a crust on the outside of the meat that adds additional flavor, and also helps the meat retain moisture as it cooks.

Don't completely remove the fatty edge from steaks or chops before cooking: it helps keep the meat moist! To keep it from curling as you cook, slice that fat every 1 inch.

Baking sausage patties on a broiler pan at 375°F helps to cut calories since the grease drips into the pan instead of going into your belly.

Don't crowd meat when cooking or it will steam instead of rendering its fat and crisping. Leave at least an inch between pieces.

Dust cubes of meat with flour before browning for a thicker beef stew.

Freeze bacon for a few minutes before chopping to get uniform pieces.

Get the flavor and tender meat of a rib eye steak without breaking the bank by buying a chuck eye roast and slicing it into steak-sized portions. They're from the same general area of the cow but cost half as much.

Cook the juiciest burgers by letting the patties reach room temperature as the grill heats -- but no more than 15 minutes for food safety.

If you love the taste of ham but don't like the saltiness, soak it in a little milk for 20 minutes before cooking. This works with bacon, too!

Ignore recipe instructions that tell you to rinse poultry; doing so can produce fine water droplets that spread salmonella and other food-borne illnesses to your counters, back splash and other surfaces.

Keep sausage links and patties from shrinking as they cook by dusting them with flour before frying.

Marinate meat more quickly by heating the marinade before pouring it on the meat. Don't do this with fish, though, because the hot marinade will actually cook it.

Most grocery store butchers are happy to do certain food preparation free of charge. Have your butcher butterfly thick chicken breasts, spatchcock whole chickens, slice ribs extra-thin for Korean-style BBQ, or even "French" the bone-end of lamb chops.

Minced mushrooms are a great way to extend ground beef so you can use less. They've got the same meaty texture and no saturated fat, plus they contain a variety of vitamins and minerals your body needs.

Press your thumb into one side of a burger patty before grilling or frying to keep the meat from bulging as it cooks.

Rinse bacon in very cold water before frying to keep it from shrinking.

Save yourself time in the kitchen by spending an hour every weekend or two browning ground meat (beef, turkey or chicken). Freeze in bags and scoop out just what you need to make spaghetti sauce, tacos, soups and more.

Shred chicken breasts easily by transferring them straight from the oven to your stand mixer. Run the machine on medium for 30 seconds with the standard mixing attachment and you'll get perfectly shredded meat without wearing out your hands.

Substituting turkey for ground beef is a great way to save, but turkey can taste terribly dry. Add 1 teaspoon of olive oil to the meat for each pound of turkey for best flavor.

The best way to get a good sear on meat is by heating the pan on high until the rim is too hot to touch, and then reducing the heat to medium immediately before adding the meat. The pan will still be hot enough to form a nice brown crust while cooking over medium ensures it cooks fully without burning.

Unwrap raw chicken and prepare it over a baking sheet to keep contaminated juices from getting on your kitchen counter. When you're done just put the sheet right into the dishwasher so you don't spread bacteria.

Use chives or the shoots of scallions to tie stuffed chicken breasts for an attractive, edible presentation.

Use paper towels to pat dry chicken skin before oiling and roasting. Damp skin won't crisp or brown properly.

Wet your hands before shaping fish patties or burgers so the food doesn't stick to your skin.

When cooking boneless, skinless chicken breasts make sure they're all the same thickness for even cooking. One way to do this: lay them on a baking sheet and cover them with parchment or wax paper. Next, using the palm of your hand or a rolling pin, pound the thick end until each breast is 1/2 inch thick.

When making meatballs, shape the meat into a log and cut it every one inch so they all come out the same size.

Next time you buy fish at the store, place individual portions on double thick sheets of lightly greased aluminum foil. Add a cup of chopped vegetables to each and seal the foil in packets. Stash these in the freezer for speedy future dinners that go straight from the freezer to a 400°F oven for 30 minutes.

Why buy lunch meat when making your own is so simple? Roast a chicken breast, ham or bottom round then immediately wrap it in foil and refrigerate until cool. Next, pop the meat into the freezer for 15 minutes and you'll be able to cut thin slices perfect for sandwiches.

Lesser-known cuts of meat are some of the best deals at Farmer's Markets and butchers. Tough cuts become tender in the slow cooker, while things like chicken necks and pig trotters make delicious broths.

Get the grit out of clams and mussels before cooking by soaking them in a bowl of water with a handful of cornmeal mix in. The shellfish will take in the cornmeal and, because it irritates their intestinal tracts, they'll expel it along with any remaining sand.

Get the small bones out of fish fillets by putting them on an upside-down bowl. Run your clean hand along the flesh to find the bones, and pull them out with tweezers.

Shape burger patties and fish cakes gently; using a rough touch results in dense, tough food.

When buying fresh oysters or clams, store them in a bowl of crushed ice in the refrigerator and serve them that same day. By keeping them very cold you'll preserve their fresh flavor.

"Fresh" fish in the grocery store has usually been previously frozen, but the store charges more! Save money by checking out the freezer section instead.

Pasta

Always use plenty of water when boiling pasta to keep noodles from sticking together and getting gummy.

For the best flavor, cut pasta cooking time short by two minutes, drain, and stir the pasta into your sauce. The pasta will absorb the flavors of your sauce as it simmers and finishes cooking.

Never add oil to the pot when you're boiling pasta -- it keeps the sauce from clinging.

Don't rinse pasta in water after cooking; the starch on the pasta is what helps sauce cling to it!

Place a wooden spoon across the top of your water when boiling pasta to keep it from overflowing and making a sticky mess. (That doesn't mean you should set it on high and walk away, though!)

The longer pasta is cooked, the higher its glycemic index. Cook yours *al dente* to help prevent blood sugar spikes.

Produce

Don't use fresh pineapple in gelatin desserts or they won't set properly. Canned pineapple works fine, though.

Never put avocados for guacamole in the food processor or blender; that just makes goop. Chop coarsely with a knife or pastry blender, and mash lightly with the back of a fork. Leave in some avocado chunks for texture.

Be sure to eat a good breakfast before heading to the Farmer's Market so hunger doesn't make you buy more produce than you could possibly use in a week. Eating before a trip to the grocery store will help curb those impulse snack purchases, too.

Take time on your grocery-shopping day to wash and chop vegetables for soups and salads for the week, and also to repackage meat into freezer bags with marinades. By doing this kind of prep work in bulk on one afternoon you'll save time all week long.

Although mashed potatoes taste best when served right away, if you need to make them in advance you can keep them warm but still fluffy in a slow cooker.

Add a little baking soda when you're washing lettuce or other greens in the sink. Swish them around and let them soak for a few minutes before draining. The powder helps loosen any grit.

Sprinkle some salt in the bowl when you're washing leafy greens and other vegetables. Salt forces small bugs to release their grip so you can wash them away rather than eat them.

Use a small pinch of sugar when you're caramelizing onions and they'll brown faster.

Start root vegetables in cold water when cooking, but add vegetables which grow above the ground to already boiling water.

Always wash melons as soon as you bring them home from the grocery store. These fruits grow on the ground, so their rinds often carry the kind of bacteria that can cause serious food-borne illnesses. Rinsing them in a solution of equal parts water and white vinegar gets them clean and can help them last longer, too.

Bananas last longer when stored in the refrigerator. Sure, their skins will turn brown but the fruit itself will stay fresh.

Before juicing citrus fruit, wash and grate the rind. Wrap this grated zest tightly and store it in the freezer to give a bright citrus zing to baked goods and sauces.

Check if corn on the cob is ready to eat by peeling the silk back and poking a kernel with your thumbnail. If the liquid is milky, the corn is ready.

Save yourself time by chopping peppers, onions, celery and carrots in bulk. Scatter them on baking sheets and freeze until solid, then tip them into freezer bags and squeeze all the air out. Add these frozen vegetables directly to soups and stews, or defrost and drain them for use in casseroles.

Cook vegetables in as little water as possible to preserve their nutrition or, better yet, steam them.

Don't leave boiled potatoes sitting in water after you cook them or they'll just get mushy. Drain the pot, add the potatoes back to it, and cover the whole thing with a thick towel to keep the spuds warm for at least an hour.

Remove the green tops from carrots, beets, turnips or other root vegetables before refrigerating. Leaving the foliage on draws moisture out of the vegetables so they shrivel faster.

Don't store onions with your potatoes. Onions release a gas that can make potatoes sprout quickly.

Even potatoes baked in ovens need to be poked well with a fork or knife before baking. Not only will this keep them from exploding, it lets the steam out so you get the fluffiest texture.

Fresh cranberries are only available around the winter holidays in some areas, but you can enjoy them year-round if you stash unopened bags in your freezer. They have the same flavor and texture after defrosting!

Just-picked corn on the cob is the sweetest of all, but you can get that same taste with older cobs by adding a generous pinch of sugar to the water as they boil.

Gently warm milk or cream before adding it to your mashed potatoes; using it cold can make them gummy.

If you have to peel many potatoes for a crowd, keep the peeled ones from browning by putting them in a bowl of cold water.

Get berry or beet stains off your hands by scrubbing them with a mixture of salt and liquid dish soap.

If you love juicing fruits and vegetables, don't toss the pulp. Store it in the freezer, and stir it into soups, meatloaf and sauces to add fiber and nutrients.

Kale can be very difficult for some people to digest. Whenever you're making a dish using kale, be sure to use an acid like vinegar or citrus juice to help break down the tough fibers.

Stash a clean kitchen sponge in your crisper drawer to absorb humidity and help vegetables last longer.

Keep cauliflower bright white while steaming by first tossing the florets with 1 teaspoon of lemon juice.

Keep potatoes from sprouting in storage by putting an apple in the bag with them.

Store stone fruit in the refrigerator, stem-side down, to slow softening.

Cook stuffed bell peppers in muffin tins to keep them from tipping over.

Make citrus fruit easier to peel by soaking it in hot water for 10 minutes first.

Microwave lemons or limes for 10 seconds before juicing, and then roll them between your palm and the kitchen counter. This opens the sacs containing the citrus juice and allows you to get every drop.

Take the time to spin or pat dry your lettuce when making a salad. Dressing can't stick to moist leaves so you wind up using too much to get the dressing's flavor. Dry lettuce lasts longer in the refrigerator, too.

Mushrooms spoil quickly when they're exposed to light. When you get home from the store, transfer yours to a brown paper bag and keep them in the crisper drawer so they stay fresh longer.

Open bananas from the bottom up and you'll never have to deal with those nasty banana "strings" again.

Peel peaches or tomatoes quickly by cutting an X on the bottom and dropping them into a pot of boiling water for 20 to 30 seconds. When the peel starts lifting away, scoop them out with a slotted spoon and transfer them to an ice bath. Now the peel will slip away easily.

Choose broccoli that's dark green or even has a purple tinge, and look for tightly closed buds so it lasts longer. Yellow and bright green broccoli is already starting to rot.

Pineapples don't ripen once they've been picked. Choose yours carefully at the store by giving them a sniff test -- the fruitier the scent, the riper the fruit.

Set foil-wrapped potatoes in a muffin tin before baking at 400°F to speed up the process. Turn them after 15 minutes and bake for another 15.

Red onions are delicious in tossed salads but sometimes they're just too strong. Take the bite out of them by soaking slices in a bowl of cold water for 10 minutes, and then pat dry before adding to salads.

Eliminate the sulfurous smell of boiled cabbage or Brussels sprouts by tying a piece of bread in cheesecloth and adding it to the cooking water. The bread will absorb the smell and you can just toss it when you're done cooking.

Reduce tears when chopping onions by chewing gum, touching the tip of your tongue to the roof of your mouth right behind your teeth, or just storing your onions in the fridge before cutting.

Removing the seeds from vegetables like cucumbers or tomatoes will keep your tossed salads from getting watery so the leftovers stay good in the fridge for days.

Separate bananas from the bunch, and wrap their stem ends individually in plastic wrap. They'll last twice as long.

How to sneak more vegetables into your family's diet: mix shredded carrots and zucchini into things like spaghetti sauce, meatloaf, even salsa.

Soak potatoes briefly in heavily salted water before baking and they'll cook faster.

Keep tomatoes stem-side down on your counter, not the fridge. They'll stay fresh longer without turning mealy.

The easiest way to peel kiwi fruit, if you don't like that fuzzy peel, is by slicing them in half and scooping the fruit out with a spoon.

There's nothing quite like fresh guacamole, which you can enjoy year-round if you know this trick: mash them with 1 teaspoon fresh lemon juice per avocado and freeze them in muffin tins. Once solid, pop the discs out and stash them in freezer bags so you can defrost what you need to make guacamole any time of the year.

Tightly wrap celery in a sheet of aluminum foil and store it in the crisper drawer. Foil will keep the celery good for over a month!

To easily husk corn on the cob slice off both ends then roll the cob between your palm and the counter. The husk and silks will slip right off.

Wash melons and berries in a mix of 1 part white vinegar to 10 parts water as soon as you get them home, and then let them air dry fully before refrigerating. The vinegar kills mold spores so they'll easily last twice as long.

Wearing rubber gloves when you chop spicy peppers will protect your skin and keep you from later transferring the painful capsaicin to your eyes. If you don't have gloves handy, coat your hands well with oil or butter before cutting peppers then wash them in warm water when you're done.

Wilted lettuce or other vegetables can be revived by refrigerating them in a bowl filled with cold water and 2 teaspoons of sugar for two hours.

Outdoor Cookouts

Add even more flavor to your grilled foods by tossing a few sprigs of herbs on the coals as you cook. Soak the herbs in water for 5 minutes first so they smolder, not burn. Pair the herbs with the meat as you would if you were oven-roasting: rosemary with chicken, sage with pork, dill with fish, and thyme with beef.

Next time you're grilling fish, put it on top of a layer of citrus slices instead of directly onto the grill rack. The fruit will add a nice flavor and your fish won't stick to the grates.

Always wear closed-toe shoes like sneakers when grilling food. Flip-flops and sandals may look fashionable, but one stray coal or grease splatter could leave you scarred for life.

Don't baste grilled meats with BBQ or other sugar-based sauces until the final 3 minutes of grilling. Any earlier and the sauce will burn.

We've all been to parties where some rude guest "double dips" in the salsa. Keep this from happening by serving individual portions in bell pepper halves, or hollowed citrus fruit. For parties in autumn, try using mini-pumpkins!

Cut down on dishwashing after a cookout by using squares of cardboard covered in foil as serving platters. Once the party's over, everything goes into recycling and you're done!

Window clings aren't just for window decorations. Put them on drinking glasses when you throw a party so everyone can remember which glass is theirs.

Making a fancy punch for your party? Make ice cubes that are crystal-clear by boiling water and letting it cool before filling your ice cube trays.

Make one long dining table for guests by putting two or more card tables side-by-side. Slip the legs into empty cans so they don't slide apart, and then cover with a long tablecloth.

Don't just close the lid and walk away when you're done grilling. Lay down a sheet of aluminum foil on the grate to trap heat and turn any greasy bits to ash that are easy to scrape off next time you grill.

Muffin tins make great condiment holders for BBQs and cookouts. Pour ketchup, mustard, BBQ sauce and other condiments into the muffin holes, and then add a spoon to each so people can help themselves.

Next time you're serving punch to a crowd, use a muffin tin to make extra-large ice cubes. You can even freeze slices of fruit in them to make the "cubes" extra pretty.

Give your BBQ party guests everything they need in one convenient package: tuck eating utensils, drinking straws, and napkins into Mason jars which they can also drink from. Add a decorative ribbon if you like.

Got a crowd coming over? Chill drinks for all of your guests without having to trip over coolers by filling your washing machine with ice. Put bottles and cans in there and pull them out as needed. Once the party is over, let the ice melt and run a wash cycle to drain the tub.

Use colanders to cover food and protect it from flies when eating outdoors.

Wrap your gas grill's propane hose with duct tape to keep rodents from chewing through it.

Set the table the night before your cookout and cover it with a tarp or a large bed sheet fastened down with masking tape on the edges. This way you'll know you have all the glasses, tableware and other items you need, plus you'll cut down on hectic last-minute preparations.

After washing them well and air-drying, store your coolers with crumpled newspapers inside to prevent mildew and musty odors.

Salmagundi

(Salmagundi is a chopped salad, but the term is also used to refer to a hodge podge of various things. It seemed appropriate for this section of miscellaneous cooking tips.)

Keep PB&J sandwiches from getting soggy by spreading peanut butter on both slices of bread with the jelly in the middle.

You can make your own cooking spray by adding 1/2 cup olive oil and 1 tablespoon of water to a spray bottle. Shake before each use. The water helps propel the oil through the sprayer and protects against clogging.

Keep raisins from clumping in the food processor by soaking them in cold water for 10 minutes first.

Make fudge when it's not raining. Humidity in the air can keep the fudge from setting properly.

You don't have to turn on the oven to toast breadcrumbs. Scatter them on a plate, microwave them for one minute, and shake well. Repeat in 20 second bursts until golden brown. Be sure to let them cool before storing!

Print special recipes on glossy photo paper and store them in a binder or photo album. The paper repels cooking spills and water spots, while the binder will keep your family's favorites easily accessible.

Slip on some plastic bags when mixing ingredients with your hands. (The ones from the grocery store's produce section are great for this.) Your hands will stay clean and the food will, too.

Make grocery-shopping speedy by creating a list that follows the store's layout. Most grocery stores offer maps listing what's in each aisle. You can also use the store map to create a master grocery list to keep on your fridge so family members can write what they need in the correct spot.

Snacks

Freeze nuts in their shell to make shelling them easier. When frozen, the nuts pull away from the shells so you won't have as much picking to do.

Don't toss out the pickle juice left in the jar. Heat it to boiling in a pan and add baby carrots, whole green beans, even thickly sliced cucumbers. Remove from heat, let sit 5 minutes, and then store your homemade quick pickles in the refrigerator for healthy snacks.

Heat a cup of water in the microwave for a minute before microwaving popcorn and you'll get fluffy bites with fewer un-popped kernels.

Keep Popsicles from making sticky messes on hands and floors by poking the stick through a coffee filter or cupcake liner before eating.

Soften stale marshmallows by placing them in a tightly-closed plastic bag and dunking that into a sink of warm water for a few seconds.

Save those un-popped popcorn kernels in a jar. When you have 1/4 cup, pour them into a brown paper bag, fold it a few times, and microwave it for 2 minutes. Now you're getting your money's worth!

There's no need to toss stale crackers: crisp them again on a baking in a 250°F oven for a few minutes.

Soups and Stews

A sneaky way to increase the nutrition of tomato-based soups or stews: use V8 juice in place of some or all of the tomato sauce and simmer until it reaches the desired consistency.

Be sure to quickly skim away the scum that rises when you're making stock. These are the impurities in the bones and meat being released. If you don't remove them promptly they'll re-circulate back into your stock once it reaches a boil.

When blending hot soups and sauces, remove the round insert in your blender's lid and hold a thick towel over the hole to avoid painful, dangerous explosions.

Home canners: don't throw away nutrition! Strain the water from home-canned green beans, spinach and other vegetables to use in soups and stews. The water contains many nutrients released during the canning process. (Yes, you could do this with store-bought canned vegetables, but most are very high in sodium, and their cans are lined with BPA.)

Always start with cold water when making stock or broth. This slows the cooking time so you draw more nutrients out of the bones and vegetables.

When making stock, add a splash of vinegar or citrus juice, both of which are acidic and will help the bones release their nutrients and minerals.

CLEANING

Appliances

A wobbling ceiling fan will burn out its motor quickly. Solve the wobble by tightening the screws on the blade arms; they work themselves loose over time.

Check your refrigerator and freezer gaskets for a good seal by closing the door over a piece of paper that's half sticking out of the appliance. If you can slide the paper around easily, your gasket needs to be replaced.

Don't throw away coffee grounds. Add them to a shallow container and put them in your refrigerator or freezer to remove odors.

Clean grimy coffee grinders by grinding 2 tablespoons of rice then wiping the dust out.

Get burned-on coffee out of the pot by adding enough salt to cover the bottom and then pour in a cup of ice and a tablespoon of lemon juice. Swirl that around, wait an hour, and you can rinse the gunk away.

Clean dried gunk off of blender blades by adding 1 cup hot water and 1 tablespoon baking soda to the blender jar. Whir on HIGH to scour the blades then rinse well.

Get gum out of the dryer by soaking an old dryer sheet in water and placing it on the gum for 20 minutes. Scrape away the blob gently with a rubber spatula (so you don't scratch your dryer's finish). Remove any lingering residue by rubbing well with the wet dryer sheet.

Clean up pesky crumbs in your toaster oven with a pastry brush. Just make sure it's cool and unplugged first!

Hate those fingerprints on your stainless steel appliances? Buff them away with a little olive oil on a lint-free cloth.

If the gas flames on your stove are more yellow than blue it's time to clean your burners. Wait until they're cool then wipe them with warm water. Use an old toothbrush to loosen grime and the end of a toothpick to clear the holes. If the flames are still yellow it's time to call the serviceman.

Got a scorched spot on the bottom of your iron? Clean it with a paste of salt and warm water.

When your microwave is starting to stink you can easily get rid of the smell by zapping a few lemon wedges in a bowl of water for 2 minutes. This works great if you've burned popcorn in there, too!

Keep your water heater in top shape by fully draining it annually to remove buildup. Sediment that settles on the bottom can make your water heater work slower and also reduces the amount of hot water available.

It's a good idea to thoroughly clean your coffee maker at least once a month by running straight white vinegar through the machine in place of water. Pour the same vinegar through a second time, and then run three pots of plain water to rinse the vinegar out. This process removes lime buildup and other deposits that can make your coffee maker slow and ruin your brew's flavor.

Keeping your stove's burners clean helps food cook evenly and maximizes your energy efficiency. Wipe spills immediately to keep crust from forming, and give your burners a good scrub once a week.

Pick up some felt circles at the hardware store and attach them to the feet of your small appliances so they'll slide easily on your kitchen counter.

Scrub your washing machine's soap and fabric softener dispensers monthly to eliminate buildup that causes odors.

Washing your clothes in cold water might save money, but it leads to bacterial growth in your machine. Be sure to run at least one load in hot water with 1 cup of bleach OR 2 cups white vinegar once a week.

Bathrooms

An easy way to keep ring around the tub away: store a soap-dispensing dish wand in your bathroom next to the tub and keep it filled with liquid dish soap. After each bath, run the wand along the water line then give it a quick rinse. Your tub will always be sparkling clean and ready for use.

Calcium and lime build up in shower heads, particularly in hard-water areas. Not only does that reduce water flow, it can lead to serious skin problems. Get rid of these deposits by filling a plastic bag with straight white vinegar and attaching it to your shower head with a rubber band. Let it sit overnight, remove the bag, and scrub with an old toothbrush before running the water. Repeat monthly.

Get shower and sliding door tracks clean by spraying them with equal parts hot water and white vinegar. Use an old toothbrush to scrub the tracks then rinse well.

Be sure to keep a jar of disinfecting wipes under the sink in your guest bathroom. This makes it easy to give the bathroom a quick once-over when people drop by, and also allows guests to clean up after themselves if needed.

Get your bathroom fans dust-free with a blast from a can of compressed air. None handy? Use your vacuum cleaner dusting attachment instead. Dirty bathroom fans can cause house fires, so maintain yours properly!

Cleaning the bathroom immediately after someone has showered makes it easier to get up the lint, hair, and grime.

Get the perfect shower or bath temperature every time by marking your favorite setting on the faucet with a dab of nail polish. When you're ready to move, use polish remover to wipe the dab away.

Did you know water remains in the pipes of your Jacuzzi or whirlpool tub even after you've drained it? Over time, mold and mildew can build up in there. Add 1/2 cup of bleach to a full tub of hot water and run the jets for 15 minutes to remove bacteria. Drain, then fill the tub with cold water and run it another 15 minutes to rinse those pipes.

Electric toothbrushes harbor a lot of nasty bacteria. Make a weekly habit of disassembling yours for a thorough scrubbing followed by a wipe with white vinegar.

Clean hard water spots off glass shower doors by rubbing them with an old dryer sheet dipped in hot water.

Eliminate mildew in shower corners by wetting a cotton ball with rubbing alcohol and tucking it into the corner. Leave overnight and wipe away the mildew in the morning.

Clean soap scum and mildew on plastic shower curtains by running them in the washing machine on a gentle cycle. Add a couple of wash cloths to act as scrubbers, along with 1 cup vinegar and half the amount of detergent. Hang to dry.

Scour rust off chrome fixtures with a paste of 1 tablespoon lemon juice and 3 tablespoons salt.

Wipe spilled hair dye off wood cabinets with a little hydrogen peroxide.

When someone in your home has a cold or sore throat, be sure to run their toothbrush through the dishwasher, or replace it to avoid reinfection.

If you have glass shower doors, leave your doors in the center of the track when not in use. By allowing air to circulate through the shower you'll prevent mildew.

When your back is too sore to scrub the shower or tub, grab your mop instead. Spray your favorite bathroom cleaner on the tub or shower walls and use the damp mop to clean.

If your shower curtain doesn't slide easily, clean the shower rod then vigorously rub a piece of waxed paper along it.

Keep shower walls and doors spot-free by coating them with car wax and buffing it off. Water will bead and roll away for months.

Mildew grows in humid bathrooms. Reduce mildew in yours by always running the bathroom fan for at least 15 minutes following baths or showers. If you don't have a built-in fan you can buy one that clips on to towel rods or the edge of your vanity -- just be sure you're dry before plugging it in!

Need to freshen your toilet quickly? Drop an Alka Seltzer tablet into the bowl and flush once it's done fizzing.

Place a drop or two of your favorite essential oil or perfume inside the cardboard tube when you install a fresh roll of toilet paper. Every use spreads the fragrance in the air.

Remove hairspray buildup from painted bathroom walls by adding a capful of inexpensive shampoo to a spray bottle of warm water. Spray on, then and wipe the wall from the bottom up with a clean cloth.

Scrub away stains on tub surrounds with a paste made of hydrogen peroxide and baking soda. Rub in gently and rinse well.

An easy way to clean glass or porcelain bathroom accessories is by putting them in the top rack of the dishwasher.

Silence squeaky sink faucets by removing the handle and wiping a thin layer of petroleum jelly on the threads.

Soap scum and mildew can build up on shower caddies. Wash yours weekly in a sink of soapy water with a splash of vinegar added, or run it through the dishwasher on the top rack.

To remove lime buildup from faucet spouts, insert a lemon wedge for an hour then scrub away the gunk with an old toothbrush.

Cleaning tall mirrors is a breeze if you spray them with equal parts white vinegar and water, and then use a microfiber mop to dry them.

Rub a used dryer sheet over bathroom faucets to shine them quickly and repel water spots.

If hair on bathroom vanities is a problem, you can pick it up quickly with a damp dryer sheet. As a bonus, it will smell like you cleaned the whole bathroom.

Keep a blackboard eraser in a bathroom drawer and teach kids to use it to buff away water spots on the mirror when they're done brushing their teeth.

Dirty hair brushes transfer oils to clean hair. To wash your brush, first drag a comb through the bristles to remove stray hairs. Then, fill a sink with warm water, 2 tablespoons baking soda, and a small squirt of shampoo. Swish your brushes in the sink to dislodge dead skin, body oils and product buildup. Rinse well and air dry.

Keep your blow dryer in top shape by cleaning the intake grill regularly with an old toothbrush.

Bedrooms

Although you can't flip a pillow-top mattress, you can still ensure even wear by rotating it head to foot every season.

If your bed is squeaky, try removing the slats and wrapping their ends in old rags before putting them back in place. Many times the squeak is just the wood slat rubbing against the metal frame.

Just because you like snacking in bed doesn't mean you have to sleep in crumbs. Stash a lint roller in your nightstand and run it over your sheets to get them crumb-free again.

Keep your bed pillows fresh between launderings by placing them in the sun for an afternoon to dry up sweat and kill both dust mites and mold spores.

Not sure if it's time to replace your bed pillow? Here's an easy way to check: fold the pillow in half then let go. If it stays folded, it's time for a new one.

Make your bed every morning. Not only will your room look neater but you'll start the day productively.

Run bedspreads, comforters and decorative pillows through the dryer on the no- or low-heat setting between launderings to remove dust, dead skin flakes and pet hair.

Make your own non-toxic linen spray by adding 6 drops of your favorite essential oil and 1/4 cup of water to a spray bottle.

Night owls can keep sunlight from waking them up too early by closing their drapes when it's still daylight. This way you'll see where light might seep through and can fix it so your room stays nice and dark.

Mattresses begin to smell stale thanks to the accumulation of sweat and body oils. Freshen yours by generously sprinkling it with baking soda and waiting a half-hour before vacuuming it away.

Owners of king-sized beds know how frustrating their fitted sheets can be. Here's how to always get the fitted sheet on the right way the first time: stand at the foot of the bed and look at the headboard. Now, look at your sheet's corners. The corner with the tag inside it goes on the upper left.

Tired of struggling with your hanging clothes? Run a piece of wax paper along the closet rod and your hangers will slide smoothly.

Add a few sticks of chalk to your jewelry drawer to keep your baubles from tarnishing.

Bring the sparkle back to your gold or silver jewelry by scrubbing it with a paste of baking soda and hydrogen peroxide.

Cars

Change your car's air filter every 8,000 miles for maximum efficiency. A dirty filter can reduce your mileage by 10% or more.

If your car has an ashtray that you don't use, fill it with baking soda to keep your car smelling fresh. Vacuum the powder away when you clean your car and refill it.

Keep an old toothbrush in your glove compartment to get dust out of dashboard crevices.

Long road trips lead to windshields crusted with dead bugs. Get yours clean by pouring club soda on the glass. The fizz helps loosen the gunk so it's easier to scrub away.

Since most odors rise (especially smoke), be sure to vacuum the interior roof of your car when cleaning.

Door locks often get coated with ice during snow storms. Protect yours by covering them with a flat magnet if there's snow in the forecast.

Loosen dead bugs from the front of your car and its headlights by rubbing them with a damp dryer sheet, and then you can just hose them off. Even used sheets have enough lubricant left to do the job.

Stash a blackboard eraser in your car's glove compartment or console to wipe away window fog and condensation. It works better than your sleeve!

Keep a microfiber cloth under your driver's seat. Next time you're stuck in traffic or waiting in the school pickup lane, use the cloth to give your dashboard and cup holders a quick dusting.

A light coating of WD-40 on your car door's rubber gasket will keep it from freezing closed in the winter.

A quick way to defrost ice-covered car windows is by using rubbing alcohol: pour it on and wait a few minutes while the alcohol loosens the ice, and then you can easily scrape it away.

Believe it or not, thieves are stealing car registration stickers right off license plates these days! Keep them from getting yours by scoring it with a box cutter. They won't bother sticking around to pull all of the pieces off.

Car interiors can get painfully hot in the summer. Stash a pair of heatproof silicone oven gloves in your car to avoid burning your hands on the steering wheel, stick shift and other surfaces.

Don't let your gas tank get more than 3/4 empty. Any lower makes your fuel-injector system work hard and wears it out fast.

Here's a great way to stay prepared for unexpected rain: tuck a couple of folded towels into a pillowcase and keep them in your car. You'll have something to dry off with, and in the meantime your kids will have a soft pillow for long car rides.

Hide small scratches on your car's finish by rubbing them with a matching crayon. Buff away any excess wax with a soft cloth.

Ready to get rid of that old bumper sticker? Coat it heavily with cooking oil, wait 30 minutes, and then aim a hot hair dryer at it while you peel the sticker away starting at a corner.

Three things to keep in your car if you're a commuter: a bottle of water, a bottle of aspirin, and a pair of comfortable shoes. Used individually or together they can turn a horrible commute into a bearable one.

Dishes, Glasses, Pots and Pans

A wad of aluminum foil makes a great scrubber to get burned food off your pots and pans, as long as they're not non-stick.

Boil apple peels in to brighten and restore the luster of discolored aluminum pots.

Eliminate odors in plastic storage containers by submerging them in a sink full of hot water and 1/2 cup baking soda for 30 minutes. Rinse well, dry, and the odor's gone.

Clean food-encrusted cookware by filling it with hot water then adding a dryer sheet. It doesn't even need to be a new one. Let that soak overnight and the burnt food will come right off.

Cold water is best for cleaning up after you've scrambled eggs. Hot water bonds the egg protein to the pan.

Also use cold water to clean after making oatmeal or potatoes. Hot water toughens the starch and makes it harder to clean.

Cut through really stubborn grease on plastic food containers by adding 1 cup of vinegar to the dishwater.

Get stains out of coffee and tea mugs with lemon juice. Squeeze it on, let sit for 5 minutes and then sprinkle in some baking soda to scrub the stains away.

Get copper-bottomed pans shining again with a paste made from equal parts salt, white vinegar and white flour. Scrub it on, rinse it off and buff it dry.

If your dishwasher has left a white film on your drinking glasses, fill a sink with hot water and add 2 cups white vinegar. Let the glasses sit 5 minutes then rinse. Prevent future filming by adding 1 tablespoon citric acid with the detergent when you run a load of dishes.

When drinking glasses get stuck together you can easily separate them by filling the top glass with cold water and dunking the bottom glass in warm water. The different water temperatures cause one glass to slightly shrink and the other to expand so they'll slide apart easily.

Get stains out of coffee and tea mugs with lemon juice. Let sit for 5 minutes then sprinkle in some baking soda, rub and rinse well.

If your drinking glasses are starting to smell funky, soak them in a sink of hot water and 3 cups white vinegar for 20 minutes. Rinse and dry with a lint-free towel.

If the handle to your slow-cooker's lid breaks, you don't necessarily have to buy a new one. Replace the handle with a wine cork and a screw. The cork is heat-resistant so you won't burn your hands when lifting it.

Make a homemade scouring powder using equal parts table salt and baking soda. Stash this in an old shaker bottle and use to clean pots and pans, even sinks.

Put a thick towel on the bottom of your sink to prevent chips when washing delicate china and decorative items.

Make a paste from ketchup and salt and use it to scour copper pans. Let it sit for 15 minutes then rinse with warm water. Buff dry.

Remove cutlery marks from dinner plates with a paste of cream of tartar and water.

Never, ever soak a cast iron skillet to loosen burned-on food. Instead, bring 2 cups vinegar and 1 cup salt to a boil in the skillet then remove it from heat. After 10-15 minutes you can scrub the food away, but be sure to re-season it!

Stubborn lipstick stains on your drink ware? Scrub with a paste of salt and water and even the 24-hour stuff will come right off.

Sure, you could leave that casserole dish with baked on food soaking in the sink overnight and wake up to it in the morning, OR you could pour 2 cups of boiling vinegar in it, wait 10 minutes, and scrub the food away.

There's a way to remove those cooked-on greasy spots from your baking sheets, but it's smelly. Put them in a trash bag and pour a bottle of ammonia over them. Seal it tightly and let it sit overnight (preferably outside). The next day, pull the cookware out of the bag, wash it well, and watch as the stains slide right off.

Use a potato and salt to get rust spots off knives and tableware. Cut the potato in half and dip it in the salt then scrub the spots away.

Don't wash stainless steel cooking knives in the dishwasher. Not only does this cause rust spots, but the abrasion of food particles whirring around in the washer can dull your knives.

Don't subject your pots and pans to extreme temperature swings. Place hot pans on potholders instead of cold kitchen counters. Let hot pans cool before washing, and don't switch from a hot wash to a cold rinse.

Temperature swings can warp the metal so your food won't cook evenly.

Dust

Feather dusters may be cute in a retro sort of way, but they are awful at actually removing dust from your home. Use a damp microfiber cloth instead, and rinse it repeatedly as you clean.

Get the dust off wicker baskets by vacuuming them with the brush attachment.

Before you dust and vacuum, give your curtains a good shake. Wait 10 minutes as the dust settles onto furniture and floors, and then you can clean it away.

It's estimated that up to 80% of the dust in our homes came in on the bottoms of our shoes! Placing floor mats both inside and out at each entrance to your home can dramatically reduce household dust. Shake the mats daily and hose them down regularly to keep them clean.

Dust your TV and computer screens with a used dryer sheet to repel dust for days.

Change your HVAC's air filter every three months to maximize its efficiency. If someone in your home has allergies, change the filter monthly. Worried about the cost? You can buy washable filters that last for years.

Reduce indoor dust by running your whole house fan a few minutes each day, even if you don't like to run the AC or heat. By circulating your home's air through the HVAC filter, you'll remove a considerable amount of dust, pollen and dander.

Use a lint roller to remove pet hair and dust from speaker screens.

The top few inches of curtains and drapes are the dustiest. Use your vacuum's brush attachment weekly to clean them.

Can't reach high enough to clear away cobwebs? Slip a sock over the end of a broom and use it to brush the things away.

Don't forget the walls when you're dusting! It's amazing how much dust they accumulate, especially if you've got textured paint or wallpaper.

Wipe dusty blinds with an old dryer sheet to remove dust. As a bonus, the anti-static properties of the dryer sheet will help keep your blinds dust-free a bit longer.

Those unmatched socks that come out of the dryer have a purpose after all: slip them on your hand to dust furniture, then toss them back in the wash. You never know when their mate will appear!

Get dust mops clean without triggering your allergies by fastening a plastic bag around the mop end and shaking vigorously. The dust will fall into the bag so you can just slip it off and toss it in the trash.

Wipe the dust off of indoor plant leaves at least once a season. Dust can reduce the amount of light reaching the plant and stunt its growth. Use a damp cloth, or dust and shine them at the same time using the yellow part of a banana peel.

Dust silk flowers by putting them in a paper bag with 1/4 cup table salt. Close the bag and shake well. The salt dislodges the dust.

Reduce sooty dust when you're cleaning the fireplace by sprinkling the ashes with damp coffee grounds first. The grounds will weigh down the ash and make it easier for you to clear them without spreading soot all over the house.

Floors

Replace your mop's sponge head every month to keep it from spreading bacteria all over your floors.

Treat greasy spills on your carpet with cornstarch or baking soda: rub it in well then let it sit for 24 hours before vacuuming.

Slip plastic bags over the legs of your furniture before shampooing your carpet. This will protect your furniture from moisture and also makes it easy to move.

Too much static electricity in your house? First, make sure your indoor humidity is between 40 and 50%. If you're still getting shocks, fill a spray bottle with 1/2 cup hair conditioner and 3 cups water, and give your carpets a light misting. The conditioner will cut the static, and your house will smell great, too.

Stubborn carpet stains lift away easily with this trick: spray them with a solution of 1 part ammonia and 3 parts water, then cover them with a clean white cloth. Run a dry iron on medium setting over the stain, rotating the cloth constantly as you work. As the ammonia water turns to steam it will pull the stain out of your carpet and into the cloth!

Rugs that slide easily on the floor are a serious hazard. Keep yours firmly in place with Velcro strips.

Silence squeaky wooden floors by sprinkling a little cornstarch between the cracks. Work it in with an old toothbrush and wipe away the rest with a cloth.

Remove floor scuffs with a paste of baking soda and water.

Never use bleach to clean linoleum or wood floors -- it can damage the finish. Use a steam cleaner, or mop with a solution of 1 part white vinegar to 3 parts water. The vinegar smell will go away as the floors dry.

Lift dents in wood floors by covering them with a wet rag and using a medium-hot iron to go over the spot until the rag dries. Keep the iron in constant motion so you don't scorch the floor's finish. The hot moisture will plump up the wood fiber and make the dent disappear.

If your carpet's high-traffic areas look dingier than the rest of the rug, work some cornstarch into the carpet fibers with a dry mop to loosen greasy dirt, and let that sit for 30 minutes before vacuuming well.

Lift ink stains out of carpet and fabric with rubbing alcohol. Apply it to a clean white cloth and dab at the stain, but don't rub! Rotate the cloth so you're constantly working with a clean spot as you transfer the stain from the carpet to your cloth. (Why a white rag? To keep from transferring dye from the cloth onto your carpet, of course.)

It's so frustrating to sweep your floor and begin mopping only to find there's still pet hair and lint that's now turning to grime. Take a moment after the first sweep to slip a flannel pillowcase over the broom, and then quickly go over your floor again to get up even the tiniest bits of hair. Or just vacuum the whole thing.

If you have young children, an old-fashioned carpet sweeper is worth every penny and works on both carpet and hard floors. Use it to pick up crumbs throughout the day rather than hauling out the vacuum cleaner each time. As a bonus, the sweeper is easy enough to use that your kids can learn to clean up after themselves!

Fluff up the dents left in your carpet after you've moved furniture by putting an ice cube in the spot. Once it's melted, use your fingers or the tines of a fork to lift the nap. Allow it to dry fully then vacuum.

Get rid of the smell of new carpet by closing all windows and doors then turning the heat up to 75°F. Leave the house for three hours, come home and turn the heat off, then leave again for another three. (Or simply leave the AC off and the windows closed while you spend a day elsewhere during the summer.) Open the doors and windows as soon as you return. The heat brings the smell out of the carpet and into the air, so when you open the windows you're letting all the smell (and built-up heat) out.

Floors should be thoroughly vacuumed, including around the base of walls, once a week. In addition to this, vacuum high-traffic areas once per person and pet living in your home to compensate for the dirt, dead skin and hair they shed.

Get rid of fleas by rubbing finely ground salt into your carpets. Let that sit 24 hours and vacuum well. Salt dehydrates live fleas and their eggs. Repeat twice for best results. But note: salt absorbs moisture, so if you live in a humid environment you'll want to leave your AC on while you do this.

Clean candle wax off of hardwood floors by first scraping away as much as you can with the edge of a credit card. Next, heat the spot gently with a blow dryer to liquefy the wax, and scrape that away, too. Get rid of any lingering residue by wiping it with a rag soaked in equal parts white vinegar and water.

Cut a hole in an old tennis ball and slip it over the end of your broom or mop to use as a scrubber for floor scuffs and tough food spills.

Apply strips of painter's tape to the bottom of your rocking chair's rockers to keep them from scratching your hard flooring.

Gadgets

Get starch buildup off the bottom of your iron by setting it to LOW then running it on a used dryer sheet.

Tired of wrestling with plastic wrap? Store it in the refrigerator. Cold plastic wrap doesn't stick to itself.

There's a reason why health inspectors check the cleanliness of can openers at restaurants: they're often coated with a thick, bacteria-laden crust of old food. Rinse yours well after each use and let it air dry. To remove crusted-on food, soak it in a cup of 1 part vinegar, 2 parts hot water for 30 minutes then scrub it well.

Garage

Clean and oil the tracks of your garage door and your automatic opener at least once a year. Gunky tracks can freeze shut at the most inconvenient times.

Nail pool noodles to your garage walls to protect your car doors from dings when you open them.

If you have a difficult time judging how far you should pull into your garage, try this: poke a hole all the way through a tennis ball then run a string through it and knot one end. Fasten the other end to your garage ceiling so it rests against your windshield when you're parked in the right place. Now you know to stop pulling in when the ball bumps the glass.

Remove oil stains on your driveway or garage floor by sprinkling them well with clay kitty litter. Let that sit for an afternoon then scoop up. Squirt the area with liquid dish soap, rub it in, and rinse with hot water.

Help door mats stay in place by running parallel lines of silicon caulking along their backs. Once dry, the caulking helps keep rugs from slipping when people wipe their feet.

At least once a year, remove everything from your garage and sweep it thoroughly: ceiling, walls, and floors. Wash the floor and scrub away stains with a stiff brush. Dirty garages attract roaches, ants, and other pests who'll make their home there... and then invade yours.

Kitchen

An easy, inexpensive way to deodorize your refrigerator is by putting a couple of drops of vanilla extract on cotton balls and tucking them out of the way.

Beets are delicious and so good for you, but they can leave horrible stains on kitchen counters. Use a dab of rubbing alcohol to lift up the stains without harming the finish.

Clean and disinfect your cutting boards by scrubbing them with half a lemon dipped into salt. Let sit 5 minutes before rinsing in hot water. The salt will scour away stains while the citric acid helps kill bacteria.

Clean dirty grout by making a paste of baking soda and water, then scrubbing with an old tooth brush. Rinse well to remove the powder's residue.

Cleaning dough off the counter when you're baking can take forever. Sprinkling salt on and scrub with a damp cloth makes it a quick task.

Freshen your disposal by whirring sliced citrus peels in it once a week.

Dropped a glass on the floor? Pick up the big chunks first, and then use a lint roller to clean those last shards and slivers.

Fix an unsteady chair by gluing a button in a matching color to the short leg.

Get a brilliant shine on tile backsplashes and counters by wiping them with rubbing alcohol.

Get a nice shine on your glass or ceramic cook top by scrubbing it with baking soda and a damp microfiber cloth. Rinse repeatedly until clean and buff dry.

Get greasy buildup off your kitchen surfaces by blasting it with a hot hair dryer: the heat loosens the grease and makes it easier to wipe away.

If your drain is running slowly, try pouring 2 cups of hot water followed by 2 cups of boiling vinegar down it. Wait 20 minutes then follow with 2 more cups of hot water. This is usually all it takes to clear through small clogs.

Does your stainless steel sink look beat up despite your best efforts? Stop by the automotive section of the hardware store and pick up some chrome polish. Follow the package directions and your sink will look brand new again.

It's an unpleasant fact: not everyone spends the proper amount of time washing their hands. Now think about those liquid soap dispensers next to your sink and what might be building up on them: juice from raw poultry, cold germs, etc. Give the dispensers a wash daily to reduce cross-contamination.

Just about everyone has left the bread bag too close to the toaster or accidentally set a plastic container on top of a hot stove. To get rid of the melted plastic, let everything cool completely then rub the spot with acetone-based nail polish remover. Use the edge of a spoon to scrape up the plastic as the acetone softens it. Rinse well with water when you're done.

Keep fruit flies from breeding in your drains by pouring boiling water down them daily. This clears away the soap residue and grease that attract the flies.

Protect wooden cutting boards and spoons by rubbing them well with mineral oil and letting that soak in overnight before wiping away the excess. This moisturizes and seals the wood so it doesn't split, and also keeps it from absorbing food stains and odors. Also: never, ever put your wood spoons through the dishwasher!

Kitchen sponges are bacterial breeding grounds. Keep yours safe by wetting it thoroughly and microwaving it for 2 minutes every day. No microwave? Dunk it in a solution of 1 part bleach to 10 parts water for 5 minutes, squeeze well, and then let it air dry.

Plan your schedule so you can clean out the refrigerator the night before you go grocery shopping. Turn leftovers into a casserole or soup for dinner that night, and discard anything that's expired. Wipe the shelves down, add a fresh paper towel to the produce bin, and the fridge is ready for your purchases.

Make it easier to clean the top of your refrigerator by covering it with a layer of wax paper that you can toss and replace as needed. To reduce waste, use a decorative towel or tablecloth you can put through the wash instead.

Place a piece of newspaper sprinkled with baking soda in the bottom of your kitchen trash can to catch drips and control odors between cleanings.

Refrigerator in-door water dispensers are wonderful, but those trays can accumulate some nasty looking deposits. Get rid of them by scrubbing with a lemon wedge dipped in baking soda. Let sit 5 minutes then rinse in warm water and buff dry.

Purge grimy stains from your kitchen sponge by soaking it in heavily salted water overnight.

Rub a very thin layer of car wax on your electric stovetop around the burner eyes to keep them from getting discolored and grimy when you cook. (Don't use this on smooth-top or gas stoves!)

Scour your garbage disposal blades by pouring 1/2 cup salt down the drain and running the disposer with hot water for a minute to remove grime.

Use table salt to remove greasy stains and water spots from your stainless steel sink, and then wash it with soapy water. Buff it dry, and then coat the sink with a thin layer of olive oil to keep it spot free and shiny.

Screw the top of a spray bottle directly onto a bottle of hydrogen peroxide. Keep one in the kitchen to disinfect cutting boards, counters, and sinks.

Sprinkle salt liberally over fresh spills in the oven. As it cools, the salt will absorb the spill so it's easier to wipe away.

Stop fighting with your kitchen garbage can to get the bag out. Drill a few holes on the sides of the can near the bottom and your bags will slip out easily.

Get the sour smell out of washcloths and cleaning rags by soaking them overnight in a bucket filled with a quart of warm water and 1 cup of baking soda.

Tired of hearing your cupboards slam? Slice thin circles off the ends of a wine cork and glue them inside the corners of the cupboard door.

Lightly coat the edges of clean oven racks with vegetable oil and they'll slide more easily.

Living Room

Give your fireplace a good scrubbing to minimize dust and eliminate the smell of stale ash. Here's how: line the hearth with newspapers, and then mix equal parts household ammonia, hot water, and Borax. Use this to wash the sooty parts and follow with plain water to rinse.

Textured ceilings, also known as "popcorn" or "cottage cheese ceilings," accumulate a frightening amount of dust. Use a long-handled extension duster to clean them each season.

An easy way to clean very greasy, dirty blinds is by taking them down and adding them to a bathtub filled with hot water, a little dish soap, and 2 cups of white vinegar. Let them sit for 30 minutes then drain the tub and run the shower to rinse the blinds. Hang them over the shower rod to dry.

Throw pillows don't launder very well. Get yours dust free by placing them in a large plastic bag. Insert your vacuum cleaner hose attachment and hold the bag tightly around it to suck out all the dust.

Keep windows and drawers from sticking by running the end of a wax candle on the tracks.

Use an old toothbrush and a little warm olive oil to get rid of dust that's built up in crevices of carved furniture. Once clean and dry, be sure to vacuum the furniture regularly using the dust brush attachment to keep that build-up from coming back.

Dust the tops and spines of books on your shelves when you clean. Once a year, remove each book from the shelf and give it a good wipe all over to keep your treasured books in shape.

If you have a picture hanging on the wall that just won't stay straight, try wrapping a piece of masking tape at the exact center of the wire. The tape adds traction so the picture won't slip.

Clean grimy shutters by wetting a rag with rubbing alcohol then wrapping it around a kitchen spatula so you can get in those tight spots. (It's important to use a white rag so you don't transfer dye from the fabric to your shutter.)

Buff small stains on suede fabrics and furniture lightly with a nail file to remove them.

Use a dab of vegetable oil to silence squeaky doors.

Miscellaneous

Clean as you go so you don't have to spend an entire day cleaning house: wipe counters after cooking; rinse sinks after using; and wipe showers and tubs after bathing.

Wash dirty carafes and thermoses by pouring some raw rice or crushed eggshells inside and adding warm water plus a drop of dish soap. Close the top, shake to dislodge buildup, and rinse.

Clean glasses and sunglasses with a little hand sanitizer to get them grease-free.

Use a pencil eraser on the metal contact points and battery terminals of your cordless gadgets to help them charge faster.

An easy way to clean stained flower vases is by filling them with warm water and adding a denture tablet. Let soak for an hour then rinse.

Reading a good book in the bathtub is a wonderful way to relax. If your book gets wet, don't fret: dust the pages with cornstarch and place them in the sun for the day. Shake the cornstarch out once it's dry and the pages will be like new.

The "prong" side of Velcro often collects lint and dirt. Clean it by tightly pressing a piece of duct tape on top and pulling it off quickly to lift the mess away.

Don't walk around empty-handed. If you have to get off the sofa to go to the kitchen, for example, look around for something that belongs in a different room and put it away while you're up. Those extra few steps add up to a lot of decluttering.

Cleaning "top to bottom" means dusting ceilings and ceiling fans first, window coverings and sills next, and then furniture. Finish by vacuuming the floor and emptying the trash. Now the room is clean from top to bottom.

If your kitchen scissors are starting to feel dull you can easily sharpen them by cutting through 3 layers of aluminum foil a dozen or so times. Sandpaper works, too!

Cleaning an egg that's been dropped on the floor is easier if you sprinkle it generously with salt or baking soda to soak up the mess first.

Freshen smelly suitcases by sprinkling baking soda inside and stuffing them with newspaper. Let them sit overnight then toss the paper and vacuum the baking soda away.

Get rid of gunk in the bottom of trash cans by filling them with hot water and adding an old dryer sheet. After a few hours you can dump the water and the gunk will rinse right away.

Eliminate musty smells in the basement by filling a coffee can with charcoal briquettes. Decorate the can if you don't like the look. Poke a few holes in the lid and the charcoal will absorb the moisture and odor. Replace monthly.

Clean that greasy coat of haze off your phone's screen with a dab of hand sanitizer and a lint-free cloth. Your phone could probably use a good disinfecting!

Get the "I served fish for dinner" smell out of your house by putting a whole lemon on the oven rack after the fish is done. Leave the door propped open a bit and the lemon scent will chase away that smell.

Fix the smell and slimy feel of bleach on your hands with a little lemon juice. Be sure to wash and moisturize afterward to keep your skin from drying out.

Eliminate that stale odor in old thermoses by filling them with warm water and adding a little baking soda. Shake and let sit overnight then rinse well.

Give marble counters a gorgeous gleam by crushing up a box of white chalk and rubbing the powder into the marble with a soft cloth. Wipe this away with a clean damp cloth and buff the counter dry.

Considering all the things they touch, it's not surprising that wallets and purses can get very germy. Clean yours regularly using a cloth dipped in rubbing alcohol or rub them down with a cleaning wipe. Spot test first!

Keep buttons, toys and other small items from falling down floor registers by placing a layer of window screen under the vent.

Hang a towel near the door in rainy weather so you can give pets and people a quick rub down before they track water and mud through your home.

If little ones have decorated your flat screen TV with crayons, you can get the marks off with a soft dry cloth and WD-40.

Put a cotton ball lightly doused with your favorite essential oil into your vacuum cleaner bag or bin to freshen the air as you clean.

Piano keys can get awfully grimy, especially if your kids are good about practicing! Clean them with rubbing alcohol to wipe away the grime without harming the finish.

Print cleaning checklists (like the ones you find on HousewifeHowTos.com) onto photo paper and hang them inside a cupboard or closet door in the appropriate room. Use a dry-erase marker to check off items as you clean so you don't skip anything, and wipe your marks off the checklist when you're done.

Remove greasy stains from leather clothing and furniture with a piece of artist's gum, a heavy-duty eraser you can find at most hobby stores.

The easiest way to clean up vomit, whether it's from a human or a pet, is by liberally covering it with baking soda to soak up the liquids and get rid of the smell. Wait a few minutes then scoop it up with a paper plate and toss.

Schedule your chores as early as possible in the day. If you wait until later, you'll find all sorts of excuses to avoid them, and once chores begin to pile up you'll feel too overwhelmed to bother.

Rubber cleaning gloves are easier to slip on if you sprinkle baking soda inside first.

Spray new wicker furniture with salt water to keep it from turning yellow over time.

Treat grease stains on fabric furniture by sprinkling them generously with cornstarch. Work the powder in with an old toothbrush and let it sit overnight so the cornstarch can absorb as much grease as possible. The next day, vacuum it up and clean any remaining stain with a warm, wet cloth and a drop of liquid dish soap.

Stale air, pet aromas, cooking odors and the scent of overflowing trash cans can all make your house seem dirtier than it is. Open the windows to air out your home when the weather is good. If someone in your home suffers allergies, do this early in the morning before plants begin releasing their pollen.

If you unwrap and let bar soap air dry for a couple of days before the first use, it will last longer while leaving less soap scum. Bonus tip: stash it in your linen closet while it dries to scent your towels and sheets.

Warm olive oil gets off the sticky residue left by price tags or tape.

Use a rubber spatula as a squeegee to clean small glass objects and windows.

Old-fashioned white toothpaste can shine decorative brass and get it gleaming again. Buff away with a dry cloth.

You're probably using more cleaning spray than you really need. For most sprays outside of the bathroom you should apply it to your cloth instead of the surface of whatever you're cleaning.

Cat litter is a great odor-absorber. To keep your closets and car smelling fresh, pour some into a plastic container and poke a few holes in the lid. Stash where the container is not likely to get knocked over, and replace every 3 months.

Your slow cooker makes a great air freshener that can also help keep your indoor humidity high during dry winter months. Fill it with water and add citrus slices, cinnamon sticks, and whole cloves. Leave it on low, uncovered, and add more water as needed.

Proper indoor humidity helps reduce dust, protects furniture, soothes skin, and can reduce the lifespan of cold and flu viruses on household surfaces. Invest in a humidifier and keep your levels between 40-50%.

Pest Control

An easy way to keep ants out of the pantry: grind dried orange peels and scatter them on the pantry shelves. Ants hate the smell of citrus and will stay away.

Trap wasps that have made it into your house by spraying them with hairspray. It will stick to their wings and send them falling to the ground where you can scoop them up with a dustpan.

Buy a large box of matches and store it near the flour in your pantry. The sulfur smell helps keep weevils away.

Ants and mice hate the smell of mint. Keep them out of your pantry by leaving opened packages of mint gum on the shelves.

Shelf paper and liner can capture both grease and crumbs, food sources that attract all sorts of pests, including cockroaches. If you can't strip your shelves to get rid of that stuff, be sure to clean it weekly with 50-50 vinegar and water so your cupboards don't become a buffet for bugs.

Dry goods like grains and flours are a common source of pantry moths. Next time you buy these at the store, slip them into plastic bags and freeze for 2 days to kill any larvae.

Get mosquitoes out of the house at night by turning on a lamp in an unoccupied room. Set a shallow bowl of water with a drop or two of liquid dish soap under the lamp and leave the light on all night. Mosquitoes will be attracted to the light's reflection the water and try to land on it to breed, but the tension created by the dish soap will drown them.

If ants, mice or cockroaches are a problem in your home, be sure you're not giving them a cozy place to live by keeping piles of newspapers, magazines and boxes around. Ditch the clutter and you'll start cutting down on pests right away.

Like to read late at night but the mosquitoes bother you? Dab a couple drops of lavender oil on your reading lamp's bulb when it's cool. Next time you're up reading, the bulb's warmth will fill your room with the scent of lavender -- and mosquitoes hate that smell.

Mice like peanut butter more than cheese, so use it to bait mouse traps.

Stuff dryer sheets anywhere you suspect mice are using to get into your home: around dryer vents and where cables enter are two notorious spots. Mice hate the smell of those sheets and won't chew through them.

Tie mothballs in old socks or mesh bags from onion wrappers and hang them near basement windows and other places where rodents try to get in. The camphor smell will keep those critters away. Just be sure kids and pets can't reach them.

Small tears in window screens can let flies and mosquitoes into your home. Repair them with clear nail polish. For large holes, it's best to just buy new screens.

Grow bay plants or scatter bay leaves on your windowsills to keep flies away.

Growing pots of basil, lemongrass, or rose geraniums near your doors and windows will keep mosquitoes and flies from entering the house.

Pets

Get the ammonia smell out of your cat's litter box by filling it with hot water and 1 cup of white vinegar. Let that sit for 30 minutes, dump it down your toilet, then rinse and dry the box before adding fresh litter.

Deodorize smelly pet cages by washing them in hot, soapy water followed by a dip in a bucket filled with equal parts vinegar and water. The vinegar kills odors without harming your pets.

Get pet hair off your furniture quickly by slipping your hand into a rubber glove and getting it lightly damp. Now you can just wipe the pet hair right off.

A little olive oil stirred into pet food can prevent hairballs and leave fur gleaming.

Get stubborn hair out of pet beds and cushions by adding a couple of microfiber cloths to the dryer next time you launder them. The microfibers will snag and pull out any hairs that didn't come out in the wash.

To keep fleas away, wash pet bedding weekly in hot water and add 1 cup white vinegar to the rinse cycle instead of fabric softener. (The chemicals in fabric softener aren't good for your pet, anyway.)

Sprinkle cornstarch on your pet's fur to loosen tangles before brushing.

Cornstarch also makes a great dry-shampoo for pets. Sprinkle it on and brush it out to remove soot, grease, burrs, and other messes our furry friends have a habit of getting into.

Give your pets a non-toxic flea bath at home by steeping 2 tablespoons of dried rosemary leaves in 2 cups of warm water. Add this along with a cup of salt to the bath and the fleas will stay away.

Hot cement and sidewalks can wreak havoc on your pets paw pads. Soothe them with a light coating of olive oil while they're asleep.

Never, ever bathe your rabbit! These animals easily drown in even shallow amounts of water. If your rabbit somehow gets dirty, use a damp washcloth to clean it.

If your pet's breath is horrible, try adding freshly chopped parsley to the food bowl. If the odor persists, get your furry friend to the vet to rule out more serious, potentially fatal dental problems.

Keep pet bowls from slipping all over the floor by putting them on top of a mesh shelf liner, or run a line of silicone caulk around the bottom ring. Both work to create traction and stop that slip.

Pets can get sunburn and skin cancer, too. If yours spends much time outdoors, or if you're planning to spend a day at the lake or beach, be sure to pick up some pet-safe sunscreen.

Train your pets to stay off furniture by laying a sheet of aluminum foil across the top. Most animals can't stand the feel of it under their paws. After a couple of weeks of this, they'll learn.

Toys

Clean toys with hydrogen peroxide instead of bleach: it's safer and still kills germs.

Tossing beloved stuffed animals into the laundry isn't always an option. To remove greasy buildup, place the critters in a bag with some cornstarch. Shake vigorously, then let sit for 30 minutes to draw out oils. Remove from the bag and brush thoroughly. Follow with a damp cloth to clean dirty smudges.

Clean dozens of plastic toys at the same time in the top rack of your dishwasher. Select a short cycle and skip the heat when drying so they don't melt. (Obviously, don't do this for toys that light up, make sounds, or otherwise involve electronics.)

Cover the hole on the bottom of bath toys with a dab of hot glue to keep water out. You'll save on messes and the toys won't develop mildew inside.

Legos stuck together? Spray them with cooking spray and they'll slip apart easily.

Walls

Get crayon marks off your walls and furniture with a paste of baking soda and water.

Remove permanent marker scribbles with a little rubbing alcohol. Don't have any around? Try hand sanitizer instead.

To get greasy fingerprints off painted walls mix 1 teaspoon each liquid dish soap and Borax in a quart of hot water. Lightly rub the greasy spots, and then follow with a cloth dipped in clean, hot water to rinse.

Another way to get greasy fingerprints off of painted walls: lightly rub a piece of white chalk over the stain and let that sit for 10 minutes while the chalk absorbs the grease. Wipe the chalk away with a warm, damp cloth and it will take the grease with it.

For greasy fingerprints on wallpaper, use white bread. Just firmly press a slice against the wall to transfer grease from the wallpaper to the bread and you're done.

Windows

Save your window washing for cloudy (but not rainy) days. On sunny days, the hot glass will streak and you'll just have to clean again.

Don't toss old phone books -- rip the pages out and use them to polish windows. They work just as well as newspaper, which gets glass clean without leaving streaks.

Scraping dry paint off of windows can be tedious. Try wiping it away with hot vinegar instead!

Dusty window screens can lead to a dusty house. Keep yours clean with regular sweeping.

To keep flies away from your windows and patio doors, clean the glass with equal parts white vinegar and water, and add a few drops of peppermint essential oil. Flies don't like the smell of mint so they'll steer clear.

Keep your windows frost-free this winter by mixing 1 cup salt into 1 liter of water and sponging it onto the glass. Squeegee away and enjoy the frost-free view. (Yes, this works in cars, too!)

Wood

Perk up dull-looking wood by wiping it with cold, strong black tea.

Get rid of white water rings on wood furniture by slathering it with petroleum jelly, full-fat mayo, or even warmed olive oil. Let sit overnight then wipe away.

Walnuts can hide scratches in wood furniture. Rub the nut meat on the scratch until it disappears. For darker woods, try coffee grounds or iodine.

If a newspaper has left a mark on your wood furniture you can get rid of the mess with a paste of baking soda and water.

Get sticky wax buildup off wood furniture with equal parts water and white vinegar. Rub it on in the direction of the wood grain then use a clean, dry cloth to wipe away the softened wax.

LAUNDRY AND CLOTHING

Basics

If you suffer from outdoor allergies, be sure to choose natural fiber clothing. Synthetics build up static that hold on to pollen and make your allergies worse.

Dabbing a little clear nail polish on the center of loose buttons can keep the threads from fraying.

Tuck a used dryer sheet in your gym bag to hide the smell of your sweaty shoes.

If you still wear nylons but hate how easily they snag, try soaking a pair in 1/2 cup salt and 1 quart water for an hour. Rinse them well then let them air dry. The saltwater toughens the fibers, making them harder to snag.

Help stubborn zippers move smoothly by rubbing them with a bar of soap.

Get rid of static that makes your dress ride up by rubbing your tights or nylons with an old dryer sheet.

Use a couple of empty cans to dry wet gloves quickly. Simply cut the bottom out of the can, slip the gloves over the other end, and place them on top of a furnace vent.

Extend the life of your kid's jeans by ironing patches inside the knees before the first wearing.

If your favorite undergarments don't come in nude you can dye white versions using brewed coffee or tea. Be sure to rinse them well in cold water before wearing or you'll smell like a cafe.

Use a hair dryer on high heat to reactivate the water-resistant coating on outdoor sports wear.

Keep a jar in the laundry room to collect spare change you find in the wash. Over time that money adds up. If nothing else, you can buy yourself a latte or glass of wine once the laundry is complete.

Need more room at the waist? Fasten the waistband of wet jeans or slacks around a baking sheet or chair back - - something at least an inch larger than your waist. Once dry, you'll have more wiggle room.

Prevent food stains on new neckties and scarves by spraying them with a little Scotch Guard.

Drying (General)

Get hand-washed clothes dry faster by rolling them in a clean towel and gently squeezing before hang-drying.

Use a dry erase marker to make notes on your washing machine about items in the load that shouldn't be transferred to the dryer.

How to dry a wet blanket quickly: run the dryer with a couple of clean towels in it for a minute then add the blanket. The warm towels and preheated dryer will pull moisture out of the blanket quickly.

If you've accidentally shrunk your favorite clothes in the dryer, there's still hope: soak them in 6 parts warm water and 1 part hair conditioner overnight. The next day, squeeze out the moisture, stretch them to proper size, and let them air dry.

Use your salad spinner to dry hand-washed lingerie quickly.

Ironing

You don't have to break out the iron to fix a wrinkled hem or collar. Use your hair straightener instead.

Get wrinkles out of a rubber or vinyl jacket with a hair dryer set on medium.

Like linen clothing but hate to iron? Hang garments while they're damp and attach several clothespins to their hems. The weight of the pins will pull out wrinkles as the fabric dries.

Get rid of stubborn clothing wrinkles by spraying the fabric lightly with white vinegar before ironing. The heat will get rid of the smell, and the vinegar will sort out that stubborn wrinkle.

Take clothes out of the dryer the instant the timer goes off. Keep hangers ready for things like blouses, dresses and slacks as they come out, and put the foldable items into your basket. Once you've hung everything in the load that needs it, move to folding the rest right away.

Shaking each item of clothing as you transfer it from washer to dryer will help reduce wrinkles, plus your clothes will dry faster. It only takes a second to shake a piece of clothing, but it takes several minutes to iron one!

Smooth items with your hands as they come out of the dryer and you can often skip ironing altogether.

Line-drying

If your homeowner's association bars permanent laundry lines you can still line-dry your duds. Just buy an umbrella-style laundry line and a heavy umbrella base, ideally they kind you fill with sand. Put the line up when you need it, and take it down when you're done.

Breezy days are the best ones to line-dry laundry since the wind will blow wrinkles out of your clothes.

You can still line-dry in the dead of winter as long as it's not raining or snowing. It will take longer, but you'll still be saving money.

Don't set up your laundry line near trees. There's nothing as frustrating as having to rewash clothes because a flock of birds pooped all over them.

Interested in line-drying clothes but short on space? Run parallel laundry lines and pin clothes between them, one corner on each line. You'll be able to dry twice as many clothes in the same amount of space.

Plastic clothes pins are cute but they're really not sturdy enough for line-drying. Opt for wood clothespins and be sure to store them indoors so they don't rust or splinter.

If your laundry line is starting to sag, take the time to tighten it. Saggy lines lead to clothes bunching in the center, and that causes wrinkles.

Linens

Sheets should be laundered at least once a week on the hottest setting to kill dust mites. Pillowcases should be washed twice as often due to hair oils that can build up.

Spray new potholders and oven mitts with laundry starch to keep them crisp and reduce food stains. Reapply after each laundering. (But don't use Scotch Guard or other similar sprays: their chemicals are highly flammable.)

An easy way to store tablecloths so they stay wrinkle-free is by hanging them on clothing hangers right after they're laundered.

Launder pillows every three months to remove body oils and dust mites. Wash 2 twin or 1 king size pillow per load, and always run them through the rinse cycle twice. Put two pillows in the dryer at a time, and add a couple of tennis balls or clean sneakers to fluff the fibers as they tumble.

Sheer curtains can really dress up a room. Get yours clean and crisp by dissolving 1 cup Epsom salt in a sink of cool water. Swish sheer panels in the salt water and hang them to dry without rinsing. They'll stay crisp and look brand new.

Shoes

In a pinch you can shine shoes with the yellow side of a banana peel. The oils give leather a nice gleam.

Deodorize smelly leather shoes by placing a tea bag inside and stuffing them full of newspaper.

Get the stink out of tennis shoes by sprinkling corn starch inside then popping them into the freezer overnight. The next morning, clap the shoes together outdoors to remove the cornstarch and it will take the odors along with it.

Slide empty 1-liter bottles into your boots or pieces of a pool noodle into your boots when you're not wearing them. Keeping your boots upright prevents excess wear on the leather and helps your closet look neater.

Stuff wet shoes with newspaper and dry them in the sun to keep them from losing their shape.

Next time you buy canvas sneakers (or wash the ones you have), give them a quick spray with laundry starch to prevent stains.

Stains

It's best to treat stains while they're fresh, and certainly before clothing has gone through the dryer. Keep a stain remover stick tied to your laundry hampers so family members can pre-treat their clothes when they get undressed.

Remove fresh deodorant streaks from your dark clothing with a damp microfiber cloth or baby wipe.

Accidentally splashing some bleach on your clothes doesn't mean you have to throw them away. Use a permanent marker in a matching shade to "dye" the light spot.

Whiten yellowing clothes by bringing 2 quarts water, 1 tablespoon salt, and 1/4 cup baking soda to boil in a large stockpot. Remove from heat, add the clothing, and let it sit for an hour. Launder as usual.

Blood stains on fabric or mattresses come out easily when you rub them with a paste made of meat tenderizer and water. The enzyme in the tenderizer breaks down protein strands, including those in blood.

Chocolate stains on clothing are difficult to remove. Make a paste of water and Borax, rub it into the stain, and let it sit for 10 minutes. Pour the hottest water that the fabric can handle through the BACK of the stain to "pull" the chocolate out. Repeat until stain disappears, and launder immediately.

Brighten vintage linens by soaking overnight in 1 gallon of lukewarm water to which you've added 1 cup salt and 1 cup baking soda. Rinse well and dry them in full sunlight, which provides additional brightening.

Chlorine bleach can make allergy, asthma and skin problems worse. Get your whites just as bright by adding 1 cup of hydrogen peroxide to the rinse instead.

Don't get suckered into adding additional detergent to heavily soiled loads: it doesn't help, and can actually make dirt stick more stubbornly to your clothes. Try a degreasing laundry aid instead: either 1 cup of white vinegar or 1 cup of Borax, along with the normal amount of detergent.

Get dried glue off clothing by soaking a rag in hot vinegar and placing it on the stain. Allow that to sit for 5 minutes then scrape the loosened glue away with the edge of a spoon. Pour the rest of the hot vinegar through the stain to remove any remaining residue, and launder immediately.

Deodorant and perspiration buildup can turn the armpits of white clothing a nasty shade of yellow. Get them bright again by spraying on a solution of 1 part hydrogen peroxide and 6 parts water. Let sit for 10 minutes then rub in a little dish detergent and launder as usual.

Get gum out of clothes by holding an ice cube on it. Break away as much as possible and allow the rest to thaw. Dip the remaining spot in a cup of hot vinegar for 10 minutes, scrub with an old toothbrush, and rinse with more hot vinegar. Launder immediately.

Greasy stains on clothing sometimes don't appear until you've put them through the washer and dryer. Lift away those stubborn stains by rubbing them on both sides with a little liquid dish soap, and wash them again in the hottest water the fabric can handle.

Remove mustard, ketchup, and BBQ sauce stains from clothing by soaking the stain in straight white vinegar.

Treat "ring around the collar" with a few drops of liquid dish soap or inexpensive shampoo. Put your hands on each side of the collar and rub the fabric together to scrub the stain then launder immediately.

Vanquish ink stains by spraying them heavily with cheap hair-spray or rubbing alcohol. (The hair spray has rubbing alcohol in it, in case you don't have any of the straight stuff on hand.) Rinse with water and repeat without drying until the stain is gone.

If lilies drop pollen on your clothes or tablecloth don't try brushing it away -- you'll only make it worse. Instead, gently smooth a piece of tape over the spot and lift it up to clean the stain.

Hot water makes blood stains almost permanent. Rinse fabric in cold water immediately to remove blood. If the stain has already set, try a little hydrogen peroxide or even meat tenderizer: both dissolve the protein strands in blood that make it stain.

Remove lipstick stains from clothing by pressing a piece of tape over the spot and lifting it away to get as much off the surface as possible. Next, dampen a white rag with rubbing alcohol and dab at the spot. Rotate the rag constantly so you're always working with a clean piece. Continue dabbing until the stain is gone then launder as usual.

Use a dab of liquid dish soap on fresh grass stains. Rub into both sides of the fabric and rinse well. For older grass stains, try scrubbing them with a little rubbing alcohol.

Stash a bottle of unscented hand-sanitizer, the kind that does NOT have aloe or other moisturizers, in your desk drawer at work. Next time you spill food or coffee on your clothing, use a dab on a tissue to clean away the stain.

Whiten perspiration-stained t-shirts by squeezing on some lemon juice and letting them sit in the sun for 20-30 minutes. Launder in hot water right away.

Use hot vinegar and an old toothbrush to scrub paint out of clothes. Scrape loosened residue away with the edge of a spoon and go back to scrubbing until it's all gone.

Storage

To keep blouses from sliding off hangers, wrap the hanger's ends with rubber bands.

Don't hang sweaters or they'll lose their shape over time. If you don't have shelf space, fold them in half vertically then drape them over the hanger's crossbar.

Leather and suede need to breathe, so don't store clothing made from these materials in plastic. Use cardboard instead.

If your clothing hangers have a habit of snagging your silk and sheer blouses, try applying a thin coat of clear nail polish to the rough spots.

Before storing clothing for the season, be sure to launder it to remove body oils which can become permanent stains over time. Laundering also gets rid of skin flakes and hair that attract clothing moths.

Store folded sheets in their matching pillow case so they stay neat on your linen closet shelves. As a bonus, you'll always know you're grabbing a complete set on sheet-changing day.

Washing

Keep apron strings from getting tangled in the wash by tying them together before laundering.

Safety pin socks together and you won't lose any in the wash.

Bleach, vinegar, and fabric softener all ruin microfiber cloths. Treat stains on your cloths with a drop of liquid dish soap. To remove smells, add 1 cup of baking soda to the wash.

Invest in a divided laundry hamper and label each section for colors, lights and whites. Teach family members to put their clothes in the proper section. It will save you time, and you'll always know when a load is ready to be washed.

Make a point to wash plastic laundry baskets and fabric laundry bags on a regular basis. Between stinky socks and other dirty clothing, those things build up a lot of bacteria and odors!

Don't overload the washing machine. The action of clothes swirling against each other is part of the agitation process that gets dirt out.

Keep tights and lingerie from snagging in the laundry by putting them in a pillow case and knotting the end. Just toss the whole thing in the wash and remove them from the pillowcase once they're clean.

Turn t-shirts with logos and appliqués inside out before laundering to protect their design.

If someone put too much detergent in your washing machine you can calm the suds with white vinegar. Stop the machine so it's not making more foam then pour 1 cup white vinegar over the mess. If that helps, continue adding vinegar until the foam is gone. Forward the wash cycle straight to rinse, and then rewash without adding any additional soap.

Remove odors and refresh clothing between dry-cleanings by misting it with vodka. As the alcohol evaporates it takes away stale smells. The alcohol smell will disappear, too!

Make your own laundry detergent by grating 1 bar of Fels Naptha soap and combining that with 1 cup each Washing Soda and Borax. Add a few drops of essential oils if you like. Use 2 tablespoons of this powder per load; it costs a fraction of what the fancy stuff does!

If you live in an area with hard water -- and 85% of households in the U.S. have it -- you may notice clothing fades quickly. This is due to mineral buildup. Soften laundry water by adding 1 cup Washing Soda to each load; it will get your clothes cleaner and also prevent buildup.

Wash jeans inside out, and only with other jeans, to protect their color and help them last longer.

Be sure to zip up pants before laundering. Open zippers can snag and ruin other clothes.

It's worth the time to turn pockets inside out before laundering. It only takes one ink pen, crayon, or tube of lip balm to ruin an entire load of clothing. Turning pockets inside out also keeps lint from building up in them.

Soften new jeans by adding 1/2 cup table salt to the water when you wash them the first time.

Wash bathroom mats in cold water with laundry detergent and 2 cups of vinegar to disinfect. Hot water breaks down the rubber backing so the mats fall apart quickly. Skip the dryer if possible and let them dry in the sun for added disinfection.

Set the color of new jeans by adding two cups of white vinegar to the wash.

Over time, black clothing starts to turn dark gray. New black clothing is also notorious for bleeding dye. Take advantage of this by washing your new black clothing with your old, fading stuff.

If you accidentally threw a red item in with the lights and now they're all pink, don't panic. Remove the red item and transfer the other clothes to a sink or tub. Fill it with lukewarm water and add two bottles of rubbing alcohol. Let this sit overnight, then drain and rinse the clothing well. Transfer them back to the washing machine, launder as usual, and the red dye will disappear. (Don't do this all in the machine, though: rubbing alcohol is flammable!)

ORGANIZING

Around the House

Store extension cords neatly by sliding them through cardboard paper towel rolls. Write the cord's length on the outside of the roll so you know which one to grab.

Maximize storage in cubby-holes and deep shelves with shelf risers: they let you get twice as much in the space.

We all get blind to clutter problems in our home. One way to overcome this "selective seeing" is by taking photos of the rooms in your house then transferring the photos to the computer where you can look at them more thoroughly. Your brain will pick out clutter. Go clean those spots.

Keep bags of groceries from sliding around in your trunk with a laundry hamper. It makes the bags easier to carry into the house, too.

Separate photos that have stuck together without ruining them by putting them into the freezer overnight. The next morning you can carefully loosen them from each other with a rubber spatula.

Storage baskets and bins are only handy if you know what's actually inside them. Adhesive chalkboard stickers and decorative gift tags make attractive labels.

Get more storage by looking up: use wall hooks for backpacks and coats; hang baskets on the wall for magazines or towels; use tiered hanging wire baskets to hold root vegetables in the kitchen; install hanging pocket organizers on the backs of doors; and hang nets in corners to hold stuffed animals. Your home has a *lot* more space than you realize!

Bathroom

Fasten a strong magnetic strip inside your bathroom cupboard's door to hold tweezers, bobby pins, even makeup brushes.

Short on shelf space? Add a shelf above your bathroom door, or several above your toilet.

Keep hair scrunchies and ponytail holders from taking over your bathroom by slipping them onto cardboard paper towel tubes instead.

Tiered dessert trays are a great way to corral clutter on your bathroom vanity, and they're attractive, too.

Kids have a hard time estimating how much (or how little) shampoo and conditioner to use. Store it in old liquid hand soap dispensers and explain that one pump is sufficient.

Repurpose an old wine rack by using it to hold rolled-up towels in the bathroom.

Slip an old muffin tin into your bathroom drawer to hold makeup and hair accessories.

Use a clean ketchup bottle to rinse your toddler's hair after shampooing and you'll have an extra hand to keep suds out of her eyes.

Kids and towel racks don't work well together. Try installing hooks instead and you'll find fewer wadded up, wet towels on the floor.

Maximize storage in your sink cabinet with the kind of vertical 3-drawer organizers you can find at dollar stores. You can fit at least two sets under most sinks. Be sure to label the drawers so you know what's in them!

Bedroom

If socks and underwear are taking over your dresser try rolling pairs together and stashing them in a transparent shoe organizer on the back of the closet door.

Having to clear your bathrobe and towel off your treadmill means you probably won't use it as often as you should. Install some hooks on a nearby wall to hang these things and keep your treadmill clear.

Make getting dressed faster by hanging similar items together. For example, put all of your dresses on one end of the hanger rod, skirts next to them, and pants next to those. Hang long-sleeved shirts separate from short-sleeved or sleeveless ones. You can get even more thorough and sort each section so similarly-colored clothing hangs together. Now getting dressed is a matter of reaching for tops and bottoms in coordinating shades.

Keep kids from rolling out of their beds by slipping a pool noodle under the fitted sheet along the edge of the bed.

If storage is at a premium in your house, invest in shallow storage containers that fit under the bed. Transparent ones are best so you can see what's inside them. Hide them behind an attractive bed skirt and no one will know they're there except you.

Choose your bedroom furniture with storage in mind. Nightstands with drawers allow you to keep frequently-used items like moisturizer and cell phone chargers handy without leaving them sitting out collecting dust.

Add a sturdy hook or two to the back of your bedroom door to hold your robe during the day and your handbag or purse at night.

Keep your car keys next to the bed at night. If you hear someone trying to break in, press your car's alarm button. Many times, that's enough to scare would-be criminals away. As a bonus, you'll also know where your keys are if you need to leave in an emergency.

Keep organizing containers from sliding around in drawers by attaching Velcro to them.

Hang a towel rod inside your closet on the door and use it to store scarves neatly.

Make it easier on yourself to find clothes for donation by turning all of your clothing hangers backwards in your closet. As you do laundry, put clothes back with their hangers facing the right way. At the end of the season you'll know which clothes you never wear. Donate those.

Keep tights and hose from becoming a jumbled mess in your drawer by storing them individually in re-sealable plastic bags. Write the details on the outside of the bag ("footless" or "very warm") so you can quickly grab the exact pair you need.

If your guest room has multiple switches for different lights and the ceiling fan all sharing the same switch plate, consider labeling them for your guest's convenience. This works great in kitchens where light and disposal switches are side-by-side, too.

Make your guest room welcoming with a basket containing sample-size toiletries, extra toothbrushes (usually free after a dental visit), spare towels and wash cloths rolled up neatly, some bottled water and even a snack. Guests will appreciate having things available to them, especially if they get hungry or thirsty after everyone's gone to bed.

Keep necklaces from tangling by slipping one end of the chain through a drinking straw then fastening the clasp.

Store pairs of earrings together by inserting the posts through the holes of a button, and then attaching the backs. You'll always be able to find both earrings when you need them.

If your alarm clock isn't loud enough in the morning, place it on a ceramic tile or mirror atop your nightstand. The hard surface will amplify the noise.

Gift Wrap

Tidy up your gift-wrapping area with a paper towel holder. Slide rolls of ribbon over an empty paper towel tube for easy but neat access.

Using a rubber band on rolls of gift-wrapping paper can damage the design. Cut a slit on the side of a cardboard paper towel or toilet tissue roll instead and slip that over the gift wrap.

Save empty gift wrapping tubes during the holiday. As you're taking your decor down, wrap holiday lights around the empty tubes for tangle-free storage.

Use a new, rolling garbage can to hold rolls of gift wrap. You can easily pull it to a table to wrap presents, then roll it back to the closet when you're done.

Store curling ribbons in jars. Poke a hole in the lid and thread the ribbon through so you can just cut off the length you need.

Kitchen

Keep plastic shopping bags from taking over your cupboard by storing them in an empty tissue box. Stash some in your car for trash duty, too!

Use milk crates to organize the contents of your deep freezer. Label the crates and store meats, frozen fruits, vegetables, leftovers, and frozen dinners separately. You'll be able to locate what you're looking for easily.

If counter space is scarce in your kitchen, consider storing small appliances on a rolling kitchen cart. Many have butcher block tops, too, so you can use them as a cutting board. When not in use, roll the cart somewhere else in the kitchen or even to another room.

Always store cast iron cookware with the lids off so moisture doesn't build up inside and cause rust.

Pick up some cork floor tiles from the hardware store and stick them inside cupboard doors. Now you have a handy place to tack favorite recipes and other papers so they don't take over your fridge.

Glue a magnet to the edge of a pen and another to the back of a small notepad. Stick both on your refrigerator and you'll always have a place to write down phone numbers and grocery lists.

Use the cardboard container from 6-packs of bottled beverages to hold rolls of aluminum foil, plastic wrap, parchment and wax papers, and also boxes of freezer and storage bags.

Utensils stored next to the stove get coated with grease and dust pretty quickly. Keep them clean, but still handy, by hanging them from hooks inside cupboard doors.

When organizing, think of your work as creating "stations" for various tasks. That means storing coffee and tea supplies near the cups and mugs, with the machines to make them nearby. Baking ingredients belong on the same shelf in the pantry. Put correspondence-related items in one place: stamps, envelopes, address and phone books, pens, stationary, greeting cards, etc. Having related items in the same location means you'll have what you need when you need it and everyone in the family will know where things belong.

When you'll be cooking a big meal like Thanksgiving dinner, read through your recipes to make sure you have all the implements you need. Then set out both your cooking *and* serving dishes, attaching a note to each to indicate what dish it's for. This way you'll know if you need to pick up more pans or trays.

If take-out menus are taking over your kitchen, glue a clothespin inside your pantry or cupboard door to hold them.

Use wallpaper samples and scraps to decorate old tissue or cereal boxes for attractive, inexpensive storage.

Little hands have a hard time holding on to grown up glasses. Give them a better grip by wrapping a few rubber bands around the glass.

Store herbs and spices in cupboards or drawers, not on a rack above the stove where exposure to heat ruins their flavor.

SAVING MONEY

Bath, Beauty and Body Care

Add 1 cup dried milk to the tub for a skin-softening bath that's particularly soothing for sunburns.

Nightly soaks in a warm tub can soothe many skin conditions. For psoriasis, add 2 cups Epsom salts and 5 drops tea tree oil, which will relieve scales and control itching. For eczema, add 1 cup ground oatmeal and 2 tablespoons honey to moisturize and soothe.

Next time you go for an eyebrow wax, bring a bottle of Visine with you. Dab it on after waxing to reduce that tell-tale redness.

If your eyeliner fades too quickly you can make it last longer by gently heating the tip with a blow-dryer before use.

Get baby-soft feet by rubbing on coconut or olive oil on them at bedtime then sleeping in socks. Sure, it's not attractive but neither are cracked heels.

If your perfume fades too quickly, rub some petroleum jelly onto your pulse points first. The jelly's oil will keep anchor your fragrance and keep it from evaporating.

Adding 1 teaspoon baking soda to the shampoo in your hand before lathering will turn your ordinary shampoo into a clarifying one. Use this once a week to remove product buildup from your hair.

Bring out auburn and chestnut tones in red or brown hair by rinsing it with cold leftover coffee. Blondes get brighter with cold chamomile tea.

Got a dandruff problem? Stash a lint roller in your purse or desk drawer for quick flake cleanup.

If your highlights have turned green from swimming in a chlorinated pool, get the tint out by washing your hair with liquid dish soap. Be sure to condition well afterwards to restore your hair's moisture balance.

Grandma might have been right when she told you to brush your hair 100 strokes a night. Although you can cut the number down, brushing does help redistribute scalp oil to the ends of your hair so your tresses stay healthy.

Protect the earpieces of your glasses next time you color your hair by wrapping them tightly in plastic wrap or foil.

Cornstarch works just as well as dry shampoo from the store. Put it in an old spice jar and sprinkle it on your roots, wait 5 minutes, then brush it out.

If you're fighting scalp psoriasis, be sure to shampoo your hair every single day, ideally with a shampoo containing tea tree oil. Daily washing is necessary to keep the scales from building up. It will help reduce the itching, too.

Rinsing the conditioner out of your hair with warm water can actually defeat the purpose as the heat dissolves and completely washes away the moisturizing ingredients. After all, that's why we use hot water to clean greasy dishes, right? Rinse your hair with cool water instead. As a bonus, cool water helps the cuticle close so your hair will be even shinier.

Keep summer from turning your hair into a greasy mess by rinsing with 1/4 cup apple cider vinegar after each wash. This brings out the shine, too. The vinegar smell will fade as your hair dries.

Protect your hair from chlorine damage in the pool by getting it wet with tap water first. Damp tresses don't soak up chlorine so a day at the pool won't dry out your strands.

Turn any shampoo into a volumizing version with a few drops of clary sage oil.

Next time you dye your hair, first rub a thin coat of coconut or olive oil around your hairline and over the tops of ears to keep skin from getting stained.

Don't wear silver jewelry if you're getting in the swimming pool or hot tub. Chlorine causes pits and can tarnish your bling.

If you have a nickel allergy but can't afford fancy jewelry, you can make any item "hypoallergenic" by coating it with clear nail polish to act as a barrier between the metal and your skin. Reapply when you see it begin to flake off.

BB and CC creams are pricey and don't come in the right shades for some skin tones. Make your own by mixing 3 parts foundation to 1 part daily moisturizer containing SPF 35. Use less foundation for more sheer coverage.

You don't need help to fasten your bracelet, you need tape! Use it to keep one end of the bracelet in place and you'll have a free hand to work the fastener.

If your mascara is starting to dry out in the tube, you can revive it by adding a couple of drops of saline solution.

Makeup removing wipes are so handy, but they're much bigger than they need to be. Make yours last longer by cutting the entire stack in half when you open the box. You'll still get clean skin, but your supply will last twice as long.

Remove a ring that's stuck by wrapping your finger with a rubber band for a few minutes. The rubber band will constrict your skin temporarily, so remove the rubber band and immediately tug the ring off.

Using lip balm when you're sick can spread germs. Apply it with a cotton swab instead.

Olive oil makes a great makeup remover, even for waterproof mascara. Keep some in a dark bottle on your bathroom vanity and massage it into your skin before washing with warm water. It helps moisturize without causing pimples, too.

Keep a plastic cup filled with rubbing alcohol in the shower and store your razor in it, blade down. The alcohol will remove buildup and prevents rust so your blade stays sharp longer.

Clear lip balm makes a great grooming tool because it's moisturizing without being visible. Use it to soothe cuticles, tame unruly eyebrows and hide those baby hairs near your hairline when you're wearing it pulled back.

Allergy sufferers should always wash their face and brush their hair at bedtime to remove pollen. Even better: take a shower before bed to open up your sinuses while you're rinsing the pollen away.

If your eyelids are itchy, the cause may be tiny mites. Sounds gross, but many people have them. Get relief by washing your eyelids with baby shampoo twice a day.

Treat dry cuticles and brittle fingernails by rubbing a little olive oil into them nightly.

If you accidentally forgot to put on deodorant, or if yours has given up early, rub some hand sanitizer in your arm pits. The alcohol will kill the bacteria causing the stink.

Keep nails bright by rubbing them with a paste of 1 tablespoon hydrogen peroxide and 2 tablespoons baking soda. Rub the paste underneath the nail, too. Rinse after 3 minutes.

If you don't like the feel of nail polish you can still give your tips that just-manicured look by rubbing them well with olive oil and buffing them with a flannel cloth. The oil helps moisturize cuticles, too.

Use a nail buffer to smooth your nails before painting them. Nail polish doesn't adhere well to rough surfaces.

If your nails are stained from dark polish worn without a base coat, soak your tips in a bowl of water with a denture tablet added.

No time to wait for your nail polish to air dry? Slide your fingertips into a bowl of icy cold water for a minute.

Use a staple remover to pry open your key ring when adding or removing keys so you don't break a nail.

Can't reach the middle of your back to apply sunscreen or lotion? Keep a wooden spoon for just this kind of thing. Rub a bit of lotion on the back of the spoon and you'll be able to apply it yourself.

Add a large pinch of sugar to your favorite facial cleanser and combine them in your palm for a gentle exfoliating scrub.

A drop of hand sanitizer can dry up a pimple overnight.

Don't like shaving cream? Smooth hair conditioner on your legs instead. You'll get a close shave, plus your legs will feel silky after they're rinsed.

Dry up pimples overnight by making a paste of crushed aspirin and water, then dabbing it on. Let it sit for 20 minutes and rinse away with very warm water. (Do NOT do this if you're allergic to aspirin!)

Get rid of rough, dry skin on your lips by scrubbing them with a washcloth when you're in the shower. Afterwards, apply your favorite lip balm or a little coconut oil to keep them smooth.

Fighting acne? Always use warm water to wash your face; it dissolves oil and unclogs pores better than cold. Once clean and dry, apply a thin layer of hydrogen peroxide to fight the bacteria that cause pimples.

If you suffer from very dry skin, give your whole body a warm oil treatment once a week. Start by gently warming 1 cup of coconut or olive oil then work it into your scalp, face, torso, limbs, and hands. It's best to do this in the bathroom standing on an old towel because you'll want to leave the oil in place for 5 to 15 minutes before washing it away with warm water. (Be careful, because oil is slippery!) Even if your skin feels moisturized after showering, follow with your favorite lotion to lock in the oil's benefits.

Keep your favorite eye cream in the refrigerator. It will stay effective longer, and the cool temperature dramatically reduces puffiness.

Going to bed with makeup on is so bad for your skin! Stash a box of makeup remover wipes in your nightstand for those evenings when you're too tired to wash your face.

Meat tenderizer can work wonders on rough patches because the enzymes that tenderize meat also lift away dead skin. Make a paste of it with a little water and rub it on, then let it dry in place. Rinse well, and follow with your favorite moisturizer.

If acne is a problem, try dissolving 1 tablespoon of Epsom salt in a cup of warm water. Spread a light layer of this solution on your trouble zone, let it sit for 10 minutes, and then rinse. Acne should begin to clear within a week with daily use.

Store a spray bottle filled with witch hazel and a few drops of rose essential oil in the refrigerator. It makes a wonderful astringent that doesn't dry out oily skin, plus it is super soothing for sunburns.

Perk up pale skin by mixing a little bronzing powder and moisturizer in the palm of your hand then applying a light layer to your face, jaw line, and neck. You'll look like you've been in the sun, but you won't have to worry about sun damage.

Tighten big pores and reduce blackheads by lightly whisking 2 egg whites with 1 tablespoon honey. Apply this to your face, allow it to dry, and then rinse with cool water. The egg whites will pull out impurities and shrink pores as they dry, and honey is a fantastic skin-soothing antibacterial.

Soothe sunburned noses by dipping a clean cloth into a cup of cool green tea and applying as a compress for 5 minutes.

Treat athlete's foot and toenail fungus by soaking your feet in equal parts white vinegar and warm water nightly for two weeks.

Use olive oil to get greasy stains and paint off of skin. Just rub it in and rinse off with warm water.

Turn your tub into a skin-softening spa by adding equal parts powdered milk and Epsom salts to the water. The milk's lactic acid sloughs away dry skin while the Epsom salts soothe sore muscles.

Use aloe vera juice mixed with lemon juice on dark spots. Apply nightly and watch them begin to fade within a week.

An inexpensive way to get dazzling white teeth: brush well, and then gargle for 30 seconds with equal parts water and hydrogen peroxide. (Don't swallow it!) You'll see brighter teeth within the week.

Used coffee grounds make an invigorating, wonderful skin exfoliant -- just mix with coconut or olive oil, rub in, and rinse with warm water. (Caffeine supposedly helps minimize the appearance of cellulite, too!)

Why pay for expensive body polishes? Mix white sugar and honey together, add a few drops of your favorite essential oil, and you've got a delicious, all-natural exfoliating scrub great for body, feet and hands.

Car and Gas

Group errands so you aren't driving back and forth across town. If possible, schedule all errands for the same day. Map the route so you're making one big loop from your home to the locations you want to go, and back.

Keep your tires properly inflated to get the most out of your gas money. Engines must work harder, and thus use more gas, to move underinflated tires. A good rule of thumb is to check them every season.

Unless your car's owner manual insists on it, don't buy premium gas. In modern engines it really doesn't do much to improve mileage, but it sure drains your wallet fast.

If you need car repairs, try to go during the middle of the week to get the best service. Mondays are usually busy dealing with emergency repairs from the weekend, while on Fridays mechanics (like the rest of us) are interested in finishing work quickly so they can get home.

Electronics

Amplify your phone or MP3 player's volume by plunking it into a short, empty glass. The circular glass will boost volume almost as well as small speakers.

Extend your printer cartridge's life by shaking it when the ink seems to run dry. Tried that already? Then break out the blow dryer and blast the cartridge for a minute on medium heat. Put the warm cartridge back in and print away.

Surge protectors are worth every penny. Even in urban areas, spikes in the electric supply do occur. Plug your computer, printer, TV, modem, router, DVD player, and cable box into surge protectors to avoid damage. As a bonus, you can also shut these things off with one switch to save money by avoiding "vampire" electricity usage.

Many times people think their ear bud headphones are dying, but they really just need to be cleaned. This style of headphones accumulates grimy wax buildup and dirt which can plug the holes and mute the sound. Clean them by removing and soaking covers in hot, soapy water. Wipe coverless buds with a cotton ball dipped in rubbing alcohol, brush lightly with an old toothbrush, and wipe dry.

Look at your computer and game console power settings. The factory defaults aren't necessarily the most wallet-friendly. Switch to power-saving modes and automatic shut-off so you're not paying to run things no one is using.

Before you buy a new printer, check its ink or toner cartridge prices. That inexpensive printer may cost more than it's worth if it burns through expensive ink quickly.

Keep your computer keyboard in top condition and prevent sticking keys by cleaning it regularly. Believe it or not, some keyboards are germier than toilets! Clean yours using a dry, soft-bristled toothbrush to dislodge crumbs, then turn it over and tap gently. (This works with laptop keyboards, too.) Follow by wiping the keys with a cotton cloth lightly soaked in rubbing alcohol to remove grime.

Food

Make a double recipe when you're cooking dinner and pack the extra immediately to eat as lunch throughout the week.

If you can't finish that bottle of wine before it goes stale (or maybe you just didn't like the wine), pour it into ice cube trays and freeze it. Use the cubes in stews, sauces, and roasts.

If you live alone or don't cook much, it doesn't make sense to buy large containers of ingredients that may go bad. When your recipe calls for just a tablespoon or two ingredients (like capers, fancy olives, dried cranberries, and Bleu or Feta cheese crumbles), check the salad bar first.

Meat is one of the most expensive items on the grocery list. When meat is on sale, buy as much as you can afford and repackage it into family-sized servings. Wrap twice in plastic wrap and add to a freezer bag to keep it good for at least 6 months. Use a vacuum sealer and it will last well over a year.

The easiest way to stretch your grocery budget: serve plenty of less-expensive side dishes and a smaller entree. Another trick: serve dinner in courses, with the entree at the end. Soups and salads are quite filling; by serving them in courses first, you'll eat less of expensive things like meat.

You've seen those long tubes of meat and cheese in the deli counter. Did you know many delis are willing to cut you a deal on the last bits, known as "bulk ends"? They're too small to use for sandwiches, but they're great in salads, soups, and casseroles.

Those 100 calorie packs are cute, but pre-portioned food costs a lot more! Buy the larger size and portion it yourself as soon as you get home from the store.

Find out when the meat department and bakery mark down foods and time your shopping trip so you're there when the prices drop.

Home Maintenance

Inspect your roof after every major storm, whether it's rain, hail or snow falling down. If shingles are missing or curled, it's time to call the roofers.

Try using a plunger to unclog your sink before calling a plumber. Many times the plunger is all you need.

Have your chimney inspected annually if you use your fireplace often, at least every three years if you use it less. Chimneys build up creosote which can clog them and cause carbon monoxide to fill your home. Bird and wasp nests, fallen leaves and roofing shingles are other things that can get in your chimney and block it, too. You'll save yourself money by ensuring maximum heat efficiency from your fireplace... and by not causing a house fire!

Are you all (sore) thumbs when hammering a nail? Use a clothespin to hold the nail in place until you've hammered it a few times.

Everyone's had the experience of taking something apart only to find they don't remember how to put it back together. Grab your phone and take photos while you're disassembling so you'll know where all the pieces go.

Recolor or dye worn leather furniture with shoe polish. Rub it in, let dry, then buff away with a clean cloth. Change the cloth often until you're able to rub without any polish coming off on the rag.

Dusty light bulbs don't give out as much light. Be sure to give yours a wipe now and then to maximize efficiency.

If your pipes start banging, you might be able to avoid an expensive plumber's visit by turning off the water main and opening all faucets until they're drained. Turn the faucets off when they've run dry, and then turn the water main back on. If the pipes still bang, it's time to call the plumber.

You can still get stripped screws out with a screwdriver; just lay a rubber band between the screwdriver and screw head.

Next time you're recaulking the sink or tub, fill the basin completely with water first to get the best seal and prevent caulk from breaking due to weight.

Use an ice cube to smooth caulk lines when you're applying them. The caulk won't stick to ice so you'll get a nice line that sets faster.

Reuse, Repurpose, Recycle

Refresh the scent of old potpourri by spraying it with vodka or rubbing alcohol. Stir well to distribute the fragrance.

Make your own dryer sheets by soaking lint-free rags in hair conditioner. Cloth baby diapers are perfect for this. Wring them out fully and allow them to dry. Each cloth is good for over 20 loads!

Reuse the plastic containers things like yogurt, cottage cheese and sour cream come in. A little acetone-based nail polish remover will get their labels off, and then you can decorate them however you like.

Those plastic mesh bags that onions and garlic come in make great pot scrubbers. They're safe for non-stick cookware, too!

Don't throw away old blinds: up-cycle them! Cut the slats into 6-inch pieces and use a permanent ink pen to make garden plant markers. They also make great straight-edges when you're painting, or when you need to draw a line around something that's curved.

Use old tights, panty hose, and nylon socks to plump up sagging throw pillows or sofa cushions.

Don't toss bubble wrap! Give it a good wash and use it to line your refrigerator's produce drawer to keep your fruits and veggies from getting bruised in storage.

Used coffee grounds make a great air freshener, especially if you love the smell of coffee. After your morning cup, pour the grounds into a bowl and leave it on the counter to fight cooking smells. Rub the same grounds into your hands after chopping garlic or onions to freshen them, too.

Buying used books is a great way to save money, but if your purchases have a musty smell it can make reading unpleasant. Put the books in a plastic bag and add a couple of used dryer sheets. Leave them alone for a few days and your books will be odor-free.

Before you toss that used dryer sheet, use it to clean your baseboards. Not only will you get rid of the dust but the anti-static coating will help repel dust and pet hair on your baseboards for another few weeks.

Don't toss old prescription medicine bottles. After removing the label, wash them well then use them to hold dressing when you take a salad to the office for lunch.

Don't pay extra for disposable razors "for women" even if they're pink or they add some fruity scent. They're the same razors that men use, but they cost twice as much, sometimes more!

Use an old prescription bottle to store quarters in your car so you always have money for toll booths.

Keep those empty breath mint tins. They're great to store spare change for toll booths, extra tissues for your purse, or even the headphones you use with your smartphone.

Did you start the garbage disposal while there was a utensil in it? Grab a nail file to smooth the utensil's edge so you don't have to toss it.

Most plastic freezer and storage bags are sturdy enough to use more than once, especially those in which you've stored dry items (cereal, crackers, etc.) Turn them inside out and wash them in soapy water, rinse, and let air dry. Now they're fine to store leftovers in the fridge. But never reuse bags that once held raw meat, anything that grew mold, or which feel greasy even after a good wash.

Don't toss that tube of ointment or lotion just because you think you've squeezed the last out. Cut the end open then cut it down the length: chances are you'll find enough for several more uses.

If the seal on an envelope won't stay closed try using a thin line of clear nail polish instead.

Stop buying paper napkins. Cloth napkins are a great choice for both comfort and saving money.

Turn a gallon milk jar into a watering can by driving a nail or push pin through the lid a few times.

Recycle old pillowcases by cutting a hole in the end and slipping them over clothes you're not wearing that season so they don't get dusty.

Instead of throwing away the last sliver of your bar soap, get the new bar wet and smash the sliver on top of it.

Plastic shopping bags make great bathroom trash can liners. Keep a stash of bags in the bottom of the can so you don't have to hunt for replacements on trash day.

Don't toss those spare socks you all find after laundry day. Keep them in your cleaning bucket to use the next time you dust. Just slip a sock over your hand, get it lightly wet, and wipe that dust away. Toss it in the laundry when you're done, and you might find its twin this time!

You don't have to throw away your favorite tea cup just because it has a chip. Cover the bottom with several layers of painter's tape, and then drill a hole through it. Remove the tape and use your tea cup as a planter with the saucer beneath it to catch any drips.

Shopping and Sales

Stock up on scented candles, gift soaps, and other small, luxury items during after-holiday sales. Stash these goodies in a cupboard to use as hostess and teacher gifts throughout the year.

Spending time with family is a wonderful part of the holidays, but so is the chance to save a small fortune on home decor and next year's holiday decorations. Make a point to head to the stores the morning after a holiday to buy decorations, serving ware, greeting cards and other items for as much as 75 percent off. You don't have to shop all day; even a quick trip can reap big savings!

Put purchases in perspective by dividing their cost by how much you earn an hour. That $150 handbag might look good at the store, but if you make $15 an hour is it *really* worth 10 hours of work?

Using a debit or credit card is just too convenient. A great way to save money is by pulling out the cash you intend to spend for the week and limiting yourself to just that. Parting with cash is painful for most of us, so you'll think through choices more carefully.

Although sunscreen goes on sale at the end of the summer, it's really not a good buy: most is already approaching its expiration date and won't be reliably effective next year.

Keep a current list of your family's sizes on your phone or in your wallet so you can buy them clothing and shoes when you find an unadvertised sale.

Given how quickly kids grow, buying them gently used clothing makes good financial sense. When the seasons change, many people sell used clothing on sites like eBay. Take advantage of this chance to save by buying clothing for *next* year. Don't forget to look for "lot" sales: you can get several outfits at the same time with only one shipping fee.

Know the standard prices for the ten items your family buys most often so you can tell a real sale from a fake one. Stock up when an item's price drops more than 20%.

Just because you don't have a lot of storage space in your home doesn't mean you can't save money buying in bulk from warehouse stores like Costco and Sam's. Get a group of friends or family together and split your bulk purchases so you all save.

Utilities

A programmable thermostat can pay for itself quickly if you set it to turn the heat down drastically two hours before bedtime, and up again an hour before your morning alarm. Residual heat and blankets can keep you warm while you're watching TV or reading before bed. If the thought of chilly sheets worries you, slip a hot water bottle under your duvet a half-hour before bedtime.

If your lamp's light bulb burns out frequently, the problem may be the wattage. Check the lamp fixture to make sure you're using the right wattage; if it's too high it's also a fire hazard!

Closing your homes windows isn't enough: you need to lock them, too. It's not just for safety -- locking ensures the windows are completely sealed against drafts and bugs.

A simple way to save on utilities: open curtains on cold sunny days to bring heat into the house, and keep them closed on hot sunny days to keep the house cool.

Check the placement of your furniture to make sure nothing is blocking air vents and cold air returns. Blocked vents keep you from getting the hot or cold air you're paying for.

Electrical outlets on exterior walls are often the source of drafts. Buy plastic child-safety plug covers and use them to keep cold air out of your house.

On days when not quite hot enough to run the AC, try placing a bowl of ice in front of a fan. The air chills as it blows across the ice and will slowly lower the temperature of that room.

Adjust your dishwashing and laundry schedules to work with your utilities, not against them. In the summer, run loads at night to avoid adding heat to your home that the AC will have to cool down. Reverse that in the winter to help give your heater a break.

Don't leave the water running when you're washing dishes by hand. You only need a few inches of water in the sink to wash or rinse. Work from cleanest to greasiest dishes and you'll get everything spic and span with much less water.

Ask your utility company if they charge less for off-peak usage. Some companies steeply discount rates at night, so doing your dishes or laundry at that time can lower your bills.

Change your ceiling fan setting in the winter to force warm air away from the ceiling and down to where you're sitting. You won't feel a breeze and you might not have to run the heat as much.

If your home's insulation leaves a lot to be desired, make a habit of shutting closets and cupboards on exterior walls.

If your tweens and teens spend too much time in the shower, it is definitely worth investing in an automatic shower timer. You'll save on water and energy, and they'll learn good conservation habits.

Running your ceiling fan, even when you have the AC on, helps you feel cooler. This means you can use a higher setting on the thermostat, too!

Make a habit of inspecting your HVAC's outdoor unit every season. Grass, plants, branches, and other items blocking the grills will reduce efficiency and may even cause your motor to burn out.

Septic systems get smelly when there aren't enough sewage-eating bacteria to handle the waste. Encourage existing beneficial bacteria to multiply by dissolving 1 pound brown sugar and 2 tablespoons dry yeast in 1 quart of hot water. Flush this down your toilet and within days the smell will disappear.

Radiators lose some of their heat to cold exterior walls behind them. Place a piece of cardboard or plywood covered with aluminum foil behind the radiator to direct heat back into the room. Make sure it doesn't touch the hot metal to reduce fire hazards.

Trim your dryer hose so it's just long enough to go between the wall and where your dryer sits. A hose that's too long reduces your dryer's efficiency and wastes money.

Save water by turning your toilets into low-flush versions by placing a tightly sealed 16- ounce bottle filled with sand into the tank. Be sure to place it on the side opposite the flapper so you don't interfere with the flushing mechanism.

Use hard woods like oak and hickory or maple in your wood-burning stove or fireplace. They give out more heat and burn longer than softer woods.

Dirty refrigerator coils make the unit run longer to keep food cool. Once a season you should pull your fridge out from the wall, unplug it, and vacuum those coils.

Twice a year, inspect your home's air ducts and seal any holes or loose joints to maximize your HVAC's output. Gaps and loose joints can reduce your efficiency by more than 20 percent.

Protect your pipes from freezing when the temperatures plunge below 20°F by leaving the sink cabinets open overnight. This allows your home's warm air to circulate around the pipes.

AND MORE!

Candles

Spray candle holders very lightly with cooking oil and the candles will slip in and out easily. Bonus: drops of melted wax clean up with just a quick wipe.

Store tapered candles in the freezer and they'll burn longer with fewer drips.

Keep tapered candles from breaking during storage by slipping them into cardboard tubes. The tubes from paper towels or gift wrap both work well.

Recycle jars that once held scented candles by microwaving them until the wax melts, and then pouring it out. Wash them well, using vinegar to get rid of the scent and wax residue, then use them for attractive storage.

Uncooked spaghetti noodles are great substitutes for fancy long matches. Light one end and use it next time you have several candles or a fire in the fireplace you want to light.

Don't use scented candles at the dinner table. The fragrance will compete with the aroma of your food and may clash unappetizingly.

Candle wicks give off a lot of smoke when they're too long. Keep yours trimmed to 1/4 inch to reduce smoke and to help your candles burn evenly.

Clean discolored or grimy candles with a flannel cloth dipped in rubbing alcohol. Let dry completely before lighting.

Did candles drip onto your best tablecloth? First, scrape away as much as you can with the edge of a spoon. Next, slip pieces of brown paper bags above and below the wax spot, and then run a warm iron over the wax to lift it from the fabric onto the paper bag. Change the paper frequently until all the wax is gone. Launder as usual and use 2 cups white vinegar in the rinse to remove any lingering wax.

Emergency Preparedness

Keep your freezer full to prolong food safety if the power goes out. An inexpensive way to do this is by filling old water or soda bottles halfway with water, screwing the lids on tightly, and freezing them. They'll continue to chill your food up to 24 hours if you lose power.

Opening the fridge or freezer during power outages causes food to defrost and spoil quickly. As soon as the power goes, grab your staples (milk, eggs, butter) and move them to a cooler filled with ice so you don't have to open the appliances until power is restored.

If you lose power to your freezer, fill it with towels and blankets right away. The added insulation can keep it at the proper temperature for 48 hours or more.

After a power outage, you don't necessarily need to toss all the food in the freezer. As soon as the power goes back on, check your appliance thermometer to make sure it's lower than 40 degrees and that each food item has ice crystals. If the answer is yes to both the food is still good.

Always keep a pair of shoes near your bed during severe weather season. If weather sirens go off in the middle of the night you don't want to waste precious time hunting for adequate footwear.

Emergency preparedness should include teaching every family member how to exit their bedrooms and other rooms in the home in case of a fire, and having an extinguisher on each floor of the house.

Find out which stores in your area sell dry ice. If the power goes out in your neighborhood you'll want to stock up to keep food in your freezer cold.

When your local municipality issues a "boil order" it includes water for dishes and cleaning. Using it straight out of the tap at that point can lead to serious illness.

If a "boil order" has been issued in your area but you need water to clean, you can use 1 teaspoon of bleach to purify 5 gallons.

If the forecast calls for snow, cover your car's side mirrors with plastic grocery bags to keep them ice-free.

Stash some heavy plastic table cloths in your emergency kit. If disaster strikes, you'll have a clean surface for food preparation. They can provide shelter, too, and aren't as heavy or bulky as tarps.

Keep $20 in your cell phone, tucked behind the phone, so you've always got cash on hand if you run out of gas, get a flat tire, or get caught at the store without your wallet. (You know you won't forget your phone!)

In an emergency, it's important that first responders can easily locate your home. Make sure your house numbers are visible from the street. Those which are at least four inches tall and reflective work best.

Some documents are very difficult to replace after a house fire. Keep birth certificates, savings bonds, marriage licenses and passports in a fire-resistant safe on the lowest level of your house.

Make sure to keep your car's gas tank full during severe weather season. Gas stations can't pump fuel if the power goes out.

Never use your gas stove or oven to heat your home in the winter, even if the power goes out. Gas produces carbon monoxide as it burns, and the buildup is usually undetectable until it reaches fatal levels.

Pour rubbing alcohol over frozen locks to quickly defrost them.

Stock up on glow sticks after Halloween. Store them in a cool, dry place to use if the lights go out.

It's a good idea to keep cash in your home for emergencies. Tennis balls offer a clever hiding place: cut a hole in one and tuck money inside. Just don't use it to play with!

First Aid and Health

Ripping off sticky bandages can be painful. Loosen them first with olive oil and they'll slip right off.

In an emergency, hand sanitizer can disinfect wounds.

Don't throw out those tiny packets of ketchup and mustard you get with fast food. Pop them in the freezer to use as cold compresses on bruises instead.

Stop swimmer's ear before it happens with this solution: boil and then cool 1 cup water and combine it in a bottle with 1 tablespoon white vinegar. Add 2 drops to each ear after swimming. The diluted vinegar kills the infection-causing bacteria without stinging.

Dab a little toothpaste on mosquito bites to soothe the itch.

Ease the itch of chigger bites by adding 2 cups of Epsom salts to a tub of warm water and soaking for 20 minutes. When you get out, dry your skin with a hair dryer and then coat the bites with petroleum jelly or coconut oil.

Apply a compress of cold, strong coffee to itchy skin for relief. Coffee contains chlorogenic acid that helps stop the itch.

Although most pharmacies are happy to add flavors to your child's medicine so it doesn't taste awful, some meds can't be safely flavored. If that's the case, give your child half a Popsicle before the medicine to numb taste buds, and offer the other half as a reward once the medicine's gone down.

Keep Fels Naptha soap in your medicine cabinet to treat poison oak and ivy rashes. Work it into lather with cool water, apply to skin, and let the foam dry in place. The lather will neutralize the oils that cause the itch.

Take pictures of prescription bottles with your camera phone so you'll always have the info to order refills, even if you run out of medicine when you're not home.

If your little one has a sore throat, give him a few marshmallows. The gelatin used to make marshmallows will lightly coat his raw throat tissues and provide gentle relief.

Don't risk losing an entire bottle of medicine when you only need a pill or two at work. Stash the tablets in an old contact case in your purse instead.

If you're prone to acid reflux or heartburn, try elevating the head of your bed 6 to 8 inches by placing bricks under your bed frame. The angle helps keep stomach acids where they belong while you sleep.

Rub a little butter on pills that are difficult to swallow and they'll go down easier. This works with your pet's pills, too.

Feel like you have a splinter but you just can't find it? Put tape on the area and yank it away to pull out the splinter.

If someone in your family is prone to poison ivy rashes, keep a spray bottle filled with 2 parts water and 1 part rubbing alcohol in the refrigerator. Spray immediately on skin exposed to the plant to neutralize urishol, the plant oil that causes rashes. Sprayed on already itchy skin, it provides soothing relief.

An easy adults-only treatment for sore throats that delivers pain relief right to the source: add a crushed aspirin to warm water and gargle. Don't use this for kids or teens: aspirin given to non-adults can lead to Reye's Syndrome.

Take some cornstarch in a shaker bottle next time you head to the beach. Sprinkle it on wet, sandy skin and you'll be able to brush the sand right off to prevent chafing.

Make your own ice packs for sprains and bruises by pouring equal parts water and rubbing alcohol, or vodka, into a zippered bag and freezing it. Since alcohol doesn't fully freeze, you'll have a soft frozen gel pack to treat injuries. Add glitter if you're worried about someone accidentally drinking it.

Need heat instead? Make your own heating pad for sore muscles by filling a sock with uncooked long-grain rice and tying the end. Add a drop or two of your favorite essential oil (lavender is nice for relaxing), then microwave it for a minute and you've got a heating pad that molds to your body.

Apple cider vinegar can take the pain out of bee stings and mosquito bites. Pour it on liberally at first, then apply as a compress as needed.

If you have arthritis, keep a supply of rubber bands in your kitchen. Wrapping a thick rubber band around a stubborn jar lid often provides enough traction that you can open it on your own. The rubber bands that come around broccoli stems are great for this.

To ease the pain of arthritic knuckles, fill a bowl with very warm olive oil and stir in several drops of cedarwood, frankincense, or myrrh essential oils. Slip your hands into the oil until it cools, and then wash them with warm water. These oils all have anti-inflammatory and pain-relieving properties, while the heat is soothing to swollen joints. You can save and reuse this mixture, too!

The hard plastic packages known as "clam shells" can be difficult to open if you have carpal tunnel or arthritis. Try using a can opener along the edge of the packaging. It's so much easier!

Get the odor out of dental retainers by soaking them in 1 part vinegar and 4 parts water overnight. Rinse well the next morning and the odor is gone.

Garden and Lawn

Just a few drops of olive or vegetable oil in your bird bath will keep mosquitoes from breeding in the water. Unlike crude oil from tankers, plant-based oils don't harm bird feathers.

Brightly colored marbles added to your birdbath will attract more feathered friends.

Get hummingbird feeders clean by putting a little raw rice and hot water in them. Swirl to dislodge the buildup, then rinse well before refilling.

Hummingbirds love their sugar-water but so do ants. Keep pests out of your feeder by rubbing the bottom and sides with olive oil. Ants can't get traction so they won't climb it.

If you hate having to stop your mower to dislodge grass clippings from the blades, try spraying them first with a little cooking spray and the clippings won't stick.

Don't put your lawn fertilizer spreader away at the end of growing season. Use it to spread salt and sand on sidewalks to keep them ice-free.

Lawns need one inch of water each week. Find out if you're giving yours the right amount by placing a clean, empty 5-ounce tuna can in the yard. When it's full, your lawn has had its inch for the week.

Keep outdoor light bulbs from rusting in their sockets (and breaking off when you try to replace them) by wiping their threads with a thin layer of petroleum jelly.

Spray your snow shovel lightly with cooking spray or WD-40 before each use to keep ice from forming while you work.

Got a patio umbrella you always have to struggle with? Spray some WD-40 on a cloth and run it along the stem to make the umbrella easy to open and close.

Spray vinegar around the edge of your pool and on cement patios to keep flies away when you're spending time outdoors. Just don't let the vinegar come in contact with plants since it can kill them.

Destroy ant hills by pouring a gallon or two of boiling water on them. Be sure to wear shoes to protect your feet!

Deter wasps from trying to build their nests under your eaves, or near your windows and doors, by spraying the area with WD-40. Reapply after every hard rain.

Get rid of snails and slugs in the garden by filling a pie tin with beer and leaving it out. The scent attracts them but the booze will kill them.

If woodpeckers are trying to peck their way into your attic or soffit, hang a metal pie plate in their favorite spot. Their own reflection will scare them away. You can remove it after a week -- the birds won't come back that season.

Keep neighborhood cats out of your garden by grinding up orange peels and sprinkling them around your plants. Felines hate the smell of citrus.

If you're the kind of person mosquitoes just love to bite, be sure to stick with light-colored, natural fabrics when you're outdoors. Dark clothing and synthetic materials trap the carbon dioxide your body releases, and that's the stuff which attracts the pests.

Stop squirrels climbing the poles and reaching your bird feeders by using a 6-inch wide PVC pipe, which is too wide for squirrels to grip, as a collar around the pole. You can paint it to match your garden decor, too.

Keep raccoons and other wild animals from rummaging through your outdoor garbage cans by spraying the cans with equal parts ammonia and water.

Next time you brush your pet's hair, scatter the strands in the garden to deter rodents.

Shake 1/2 cup flour with 2 tablespoons each of cayenne pepper and dry mustard powder. Sprinkle this around your garden's perimeter to keep squirrels away, and reapply after each rain.

Sprinkle crushed egg shells liberally around the base of plants to deter slugs and snails. Their soft underbellies can't handle crawling on the sharp edges of the shells so they'll leave your plants alone.

Save the plastic utensils from fast food restaurants to use as labels in your garden. Just write the name of plants on the handle with a permanent marker and stick them in the ground.

If your guests actually leave unfinished bottles of beer around after a party, use the brew to water your garden. Plants love the fermented sugars and the alcohol will kill fungus and mold spores.

Slip a dryer sheet through your belt loop when you're spending time outdoors to keep mosquitoes away. Those sheets are so strongly scented the pests won't be able to smell *you*!

Don't leave the dirt on your garden tools at the end of gardening season or they'll rust. Hose them off over the garden beds, dry them well, and then give them a light coating of oil, including the wood handles.

Get rid of black spot and powdery mildew on your plants by dissolving two aspirin in 1 quart of water overnight and spraying it on the plant's leaves.

Keep those banana peels: bury them at the base of rose bushes where they'll act as a wonderful fertilizer and you'll get bigger blossoms.

Don't throw away flat club soda or mineral water: feed it to your plants instead and the minerals will help them thrive! Limit to once a week, with regular water in between, to avoid sodium buildup in the soil.

Get rid of moss on cement by spraying it with straight white vinegar. Let it sit for 8 hours then scrub and rinse. Don't use this near plants, though, since vinegar can kill them.

Don't try to rush planting season. If the ground is still wet from thawed snow or rain, disturbing it can cause the soil to compact and form hard clumps which keep seedlings from sprouting and interfere with root development.

Hydrogen peroxide can help protect your plants from root rot and mildew. Add 1 ounce to every quart of water and direct your watering can toward the soil, not plant leaves.

Spread the fragrance of pine trees throughout your home by removing the needles from a branch and drying them on a towel in a shady spot for several days. Stuff a handful into the back of throw pillows, scatter some among potpourri, or simmer 1/2 cup in 3 cups of water on your stove.

Start seedlings in egg shells then just transplant the whole thing. The eggshell's calcium will fertilize the plant as it grows.

If winters are harsh where you live, be sure to add several inches of mulch around the base of your tender perennials to keep them protected against brutal temperatures.

Snip parsley plants from the center to keep them from bolting.

Keep container plants from drying out on very hot days with a cup of ice cubes sprinkled on the soil.

The water you use to boil eggs contains a lot of calcium from their shells. As long as you didn't use salt or vinegar in the water, let it cool and water your plants with it.

Spraying water on your plants when the sun is overhead can scorch tender leaves. Water at the base of plants or invest in soaker hoses instead.

Use scissors or shears to pick fruit from your trees. Yanking on the fruit shakes the tree so other fruit falls and bruises when it hits the ground.

Add fresh water to arranged bouquets with a turkey baster to avoid disturbing the arrangement.

Keep lilies from shedding pollen on your clothes and in your house by removing the stamens, or spray them with hairspray and leave them in place if you prefer that look.

Here's how to get a professional looking floral arrangement even if you're all thumbs: use tape to form a grid across the top of the vase then use another strip of tape to secure the grid's ends. Slip the tallest stems into center squares, floppier flowers on the outer edge, and fill the rest with remaining flowers and greenery.

Remove any leaves that will be below the waterline when you put a bouquet into a vase. Leaves submerged in water rot quickly; removing them will prolong the life of your floral arrangement.

Keep floral bouquets alive longer by adding half an aspirin or a shot of vodka to the water.

Never water your lawn in the heat of the day. Not only do you risk scorching the grass, you'll lose water to evaporation. Water before 8 AM instead.

Drop a bar of soap into an old plastic onion bag and attach it to your outdoor faucets for easy post-gardening clean up that keeps dirt out of your house.

Rain barrels can pay for themselves in one season provided your city allows them. They can also breed a scary number of mosquitoes, so keep yours tightly sealed. Remove them before the first hard freeze so they don't crack.

Pouring a beer over your compost heap on a weekly basis will speed the breakdown of organic matter.

Deter rodents from raiding your garden by scattering blood meal around the perimeter and in between plants. It acts as a fertilizer, too! Reapply every 2 weeks or after hard rains.

An inexpensive way to get more garden plants is by growing cuttings from the plants you already own. Dip the cuttings in a solution of 2 aspirins dissolved in water, and then pop them into moist soil or sand until roots form. The aspirin's salicylic acid acts as a growth hormone for plants and speeds the rooting process along.

At the garden center, keep your eyes open for plant containers with more than one seedling in them. If they're healthy you'll basically get two plants for the price of one.

Contact your city's sanitation department in early spring and late autumn to ask about free mulch. Many towns hold weekends when residents can bring tree trimmings and garden debris which the city then turns into mulch that's free for the asking.

Don't tug on tomatoes to pick them -- vines are fragile! Use a pair of scissors instead. Be sure they're clean to avoid spreading plant diseases.

In the autumn, let a few of your annual plants to go seed. Pick the seed pods, empty them into envelopes, and write the plant names on the outside. Next spring you can save money by growing your own.

Rake your fingernails deeply across a bar of soap before working in the garden. The soap will keep dirt from forming under your nails, and you can just wash it away when you're done.

Soak stained flower pots overnight in a bucket filled with equal parts water and white vinegar. Scrub with a stiff brush then wash with soap and water before use.

Watering the garden in the evening can spread plant disease and lead to root rot, tamping off and mildew. Water in the morning instead.

If your pool water is starting to get a layer of oil from sunscreen try tossing a few tennis balls in there. The fuzzy fibers grab on to oils. Just fish them out, rinse them off, and toss them back in to keep the pool oil-free.

Don't rush out to buy a new kiddie pool just because it's sprung a leak. Drain and dry it, then patch both sides with duct or plumber's tape, both of which adhere well under water.

Cover the springs of trampolines with pool noodles to keep fingers and toes from getting caught in them. Just slice the appropriate length, cut a slit down the edge, and slip it over the spring.

Painting

Line paint roller trays with aluminum foil to make clean-up a cinch. Once you're done working, just gather the corners of the foil together and dispose.

Forgot to rinse your paintbrush? Soften dry paint by soaking the brush for 30 minutes in hot white vinegar.

Coat light switches with glow-in-the-dark paint to make them easy to find. Little ones appreciate this almost as much as house guests do.

To clean metals before painting (besides aluminum), wipe them down with turpentine. This gets rid of oil and will help the paint adhere.

Next time you're painting, fill nail holes in the walls with white toothpaste. It's just as hard as Spackle and lasts just as long, but you won't have to run to the hardware store.

Repainting a room? Write how many gallons you used along with the brand and color on the inside of a light switch plate. Next time you'll know how much and what color paint to buy.

Stretch a thick rubber band vertically over the middle of a paint can and use it to scrape excess paint off your brush as you work. Not only will this reduce drips and keep you from applying too thick a coat, the can's rim will be clean when you're ready to close it.

Mix equal parts water and fabric softener in a spray bottle to make a solution that helps remove wall paper. Just score the paper lightly, spray the mix on and wait 15 minutes. You'll be able to peel the paper away easily. Wash the wall well with equal parts white vinegar and warm water to remove any remaining residue, and allow it to dry overnight.

To remove paint from hair, coat your strands with a little warm olive oil and wait five minutes. You should be able to slip the paint right off using only your fingers.

Safety

Do not throw a rug over an electric cord to hide it. Heat can build up, and hidden cords can be pinched or cut without your knowledge -- situations which pose great fire dangers.

Never tuck your phone under your pillow while it's charging. Phones build up heat as they charge, and but a pillow can trap that heat and start a fire.

Add a strip of glow-in-the-dark tape to the edges of your TV remote so you don't trip over it while watching movies in the dark. This also makes it easy to find, even when it falls behind the sofa.

Paint basement stairs and ladders with non-glossy paint then sprinkle on sand while the paint is still wet. Once dry, vacuum away the excess. The gritty paint adds traction so you're less likely to slip.

Most burglars are lazy and look for easy entry into target homes. Deter them by planting prickly bushes like juniper, holly, blackthorn and pine beneath your home's windows.

Unplug your garage door opener when you leave on vacation so would-be thieves can't hack the code and get into your house.

Use adhesive bath strips to make basement and deck stairs safer. They work great on stepladders, too!

Shoelaces seem to come untied at the most inconvenient times. Keep them from coming loose by rubbing a little Chapstick on the knot.

Sewing

Dull sewing needles and safety pins can be easily sharpened with an emery board.

Tack a bag to the wall or keep a separate basket in your laundry room for clothing in need of repairs. Grab it and get to work when you're watching TV, or take it along when you'll have a long wait in line in the car.

Attach magnetic strips inside the lid of your sewing box to hold bobbins.

To make threading a needle easier, spray the end of the thread with a little hairspray.

Tuck a magnet or two in your sewing basket and use it to pick up dropped pins.

ABOUT THE AUTHOR

Katie Berry has been in love with all things domestic since she first read the *Little House on the Prairie* series when she was nine years old. Though she's never made maple candy in the snow, she *has* learned a lot since then about homebody endeavors.

After a decade-long detour into the professional world, Katie followed her heart (and her husband, as the military transferred him across the country) and became a housewife. It wasn't long before she discovered that caring for two children, two pets, and a workaholic husband could keep her busy 24 hours a day if she wasn't careful. That's when she set out to learn about how to cook, clean, do laundry, get organized and save money... without losing her mind.

Now her daughter is running a household of her own, her son is in high school, and her husband is retired. Katie still considers herself a housewife but has made it her mission to share with others the tips and tricks she's stumbled across over the years.

You'll find those tips in this book and on her blog, Housewife How-To's® (HousewifeHowTos.com). She's also published a book, *30 Days to a Clean and Organized House*, which contains even more advice along with flowcharts and checklists to help you clean every nook and cranny in your home.

Made in the USA
Middletown, DE
12 December 2017